CONTENTS

Feed the World
Birhan Woldu
and Live Aid

Oliver Harvey

Foreword by
Bob Geldof

NEW
HOLLAND

FOREWORD

by

BOB GELDOF

BIRHAN IS A WONDER. She is a beautiful, clever young woman from the Northern Highlands of Ethiopia. She had originally featured as a dying infant in extreme agony in the now-famous Canadian Broadcasting Corporation (CBC) footage, which David Bowie introduced, that stopped the world cold at the Live Aid concerts of 1985. Twenty years later the world watched again as Birhan appeared as a stunning, dignified, resolute, intelligent, productive, dynamic human being alongside Madonna at the Live 8 concerts of 2005. Now she was the living proof that each life is sacred and that each individual lost is a loss to all.

Birhan's story and that of her family beggars belief. Not just that she was able to go from a subsistence life pretty much unchanged from pre-medieval times to become a glowing paradigm of an independent, college-educated, glamorous 21st-century woman in just 20 years. But also that she could go from an agonized, shrieking, shrunk, dying, little scrap of humanity cradled sorrowfully in her father's gentle arms to a glowing, ever smiling, serene woman of our time almost seems impossible.

Who was the greater star that day? Madonna or Birhan?

For the world it was clear. Here was OUR miracle. Here was the living proof that it is not futile to help. That aid most certainly works. With one smile Birhan defeated the cynics and made us understand that all of that effort had been worth it. Indeed, now, when people say to me: 'Why do you do it?', it is easy to just point at this girl and say, 'Because of that!'

And I tell you this: if, after all the years of work and effort and sleeplessness and travel and meetings and triumphs and mistakes; if, after all of the money and politics and shouting and arguing – if, after all of that, it had all only resulted in the single life of this woman, then just for that one life, just for that single human being, it would have been worth it.

Birhan survived because of Brian Stewart, a wonderful reporter for the CBC, who made the original film we showed that day at Live Aid in 1985. He made sure she was cared for and supported throughout her life. Oliver Harvey then brought her to the attention of the world again. All you can say is 'Thank God' – for her and for both of those men.

This is Birhan's extraordinary story told with profound respect and clear emotion by a man who has obviously imbibed her culture and come to love and respect it. Oliver fills his narrative with erudition and explanation. He has come to love Ethiopia – the most beautiful of lands – as does anyone who goes there.

When I first met Oliver I thought he was the most unlikely of candidates to ever 'get' what was going on. It crossed my mind that his parents had to have had a vivid sense of humour when they named him, more or less, after one of the greatest funny men of all time. Was this 'another fine mess' he was going to get me into?

Oliver was the very model of the model of the British journalist. Straight out of Evelyn Waugh. Crumpled, sweaty, dressed in an off-white linen suit and inappropriately heavy brogues. Weedy rather than skinny, blinking constantly behind thick glasses, thinning hair sweat-plastered to a damp skull and hesitantly asking frankly silly 'human-angle' tabloid questions. I saw him again a week later. Same clothes. Same sweat. Same discomfort. Different questions – this time penetrating, clever, full of understanding, curious. He was a journalist. He was hooked. Africa had got him.

It was Michael Buerk, though, who made the agony of the Great African Famines a televisual reality for us in the 1980s. Paul Vallely, now Associate Editor of the UK's *Independent* newspaper, gave us the insights and realities of the hunger through his broadsheet journalism. Oliver just helped make the individual tragedies a clearly understood reality for millions of Britons through his great tabloid reporting.

Like thousands of others who engaged with this 'story' Oliver got hooked. He realized that he could use his talents and job to achieve something greater than the momentary satisfaction of a 'good story'. He could actually help to change things. He did so by making the vast readership of *The Sun* newspaper understand and identify with the immeasurably brave souls and their torture in the parched lands of Ethiopia. As a result, no politician could safely ignore this concern.

To its undying credit and pride, Britain, despite its often difficult economic circumstances, has pledged itself – through several governments of all political hues – to maintain its promises to the poor. In this it is wholly supported by the majority of the public and the media. It is now among the world leaders in the area of development and assistance to developing countries – with all the attendant and immense benefits of 'soft power' that come with the strength of doing what you say and of holding to your political convictions.

Over the years I've seen Oliver bed down wherever there was space. Mud floors, wooden benches, low-powered mosquito-humming hot rooms, wherever. He never stands aloof. He literally seems quite at home amongst the most fantastical of peoples and actively participates in whatever is going on with them like he's having the absolute best time of his life. He is never patronizing. Rather he's laughing, chatting, accepting and being accepted and loving it.

He's a hard nut and I have a deep respect for him as a man and as a reporter. One never hears the expression 'Fleet Street's finest' any more. It has become an oxymoron. But in the unlikely circumstance that the dignity and pride of the British press is ever restored, it will be quite right to say of one O. Harvey that he is, indeed, one of Fleet Street's finest.

In this book Oliver tells the tale of his greatest story – the life of Birhan Woldu. The story of the life of a dying child, whose image so appalled the world that it could not stand by and let it pass without action. And the world has been repaid times over for its compassion. In Birhan, this glorious human being, the world has the perfect exemplar of what it is to be human and alive.

AUTHOR PREFACE

IT'S A MERE SEVEN-and-three-quarter-hour night flight from London to Ethiopia over the bumpy heat thermals of the Sahara. You land in a nation literally out of time. Setting off from a cloudy Heathrow in 2011 you touch down in capital Addis Ababa's gleaming and impressive Bole airport in 2004. Ethiopia has never switched from the Julian calendar like Europe did in 1582 and so is permanently seven years and eight months behind. You might even have landed in Ethiopia's extra month. It gives rise to the tourist board's boast of '13 months of sunshine'. The clock on the wall is confusing too. There is a 12-hour day, beginning at dawn and ending at sunset.

Ethiopia is a land apart. Tourists expecting a country of barren desert are confronted by soaring peaks, lush river valleys and reed-fringed lakes. It has been called the 'Cradle of Humanity', where modern humans first evolved. It is the world's second oldest Christian country and was never properly colonized in the Scramble for Africa. It has an ancient written language Ge'ez; there are medieval stone castles in Gonder and rock-hewn churches in the holy city of Lalibela, often described as the 'eighth wonder of the world'. The fiercely proud and profoundly religious people can look as Arabian as African.

A further hour-and-half flight from Addis brings you to Mekele in Ethiopia's mountainous north – this is the home town of Birhan Woldu. Mekele, capital of Tigray Province, is now a thriving city of over 200,000. Visible on the horizon are giant white wind turbines, which are being constructed above fields tilled by oxen-dragged wooden ploughs, a method unchanged since the Iron Age. Cement and tile factories line the Chinese-built highway. Camel trains, laden with salt blocks cut in the distant Danakil Depression, plod towards the city's market past expensive villas with satellite dishes bolted to their walls for their expat owners to catch the latest game while on vacation from London, Toronto and Seattle. In 1984 the tinder-dry plains around the city were the epicentre of the 20th century's worst humanitarian disaster. A 'biblical famine' in which an estimated one million people died. It could have been far more – nobody really knows for sure. Like thousands of others, Birhan and her family came here seeking salvation when their crops shrivelled in the sun and their grain stores emptied.

I have a dear friend, Anthony Mitchell, to thank both for introducing me to this amazing land and for helping me find the path to Birhan and her family. A former foot-in-the-door hack at Britain's *Daily Express* newspaper, Anthony had moved to Addis to be with his future wife, Catherine Fitzgibbon, who worked for Irish charity Goal and later Save the Children. In 2001 Anthony and I enjoyed a *Boy's Own* adventure, trekking and camping in the breathtakingly beautiful Simien Mountains. We hired a cook, a guide and a AK-47-toting guard while our mules were laden with wine and whisky, blankets and fresh food. Passing through the upland villages, it was the warmth, easiness and the sheer joy of living shown by the Ethiopian people that stayed with me.

AUTHOR PREFACE

When I returned to Ethiopia in 2002, to write development features for my newspaper *The Sun*, the UK's biggest-selling paper, Anthony was on hand with his by now expert knowledge of the region. In the parched Awash district in central Ethiopia I witnessed for the first time the horrific sight of proud but malnourished families queuing at feeding centres. Ethiopia still couldn't feed itself nearly 20 years after the famous Live Aid concert.

In the following year Anthony and I were both part of a press pack shadowing Bob Geldof as he criss-crossed the country. Anthony would later be forced out of Ethiopia after the government accused him of 'hostile' reporting. He would never leave his beloved Africa, however. Anthony was one of 114 people killed when Kenyan Airways flight KQ507 plunged into a mangrove swamp in Cameroon on May 5, 2007.

In September 2004 though, I had rang Anthony to ask him to help me set up an interview with Birhan Woldu who had been seen close to death in the famous film of starving children screened at Live Aid. The idea was to provide a real human story as part of a series on the 20th anniversary of Ethiopia's famine that I was writing for *The Sun*. To move away from dry development facts and convoluted aid arguments and show what one life saved really meant. Then it mushroomed into something incredible and unforeseen. Birhan's story simply resonated so strongly.

First there had been an emotion-charged meeting arranged by my paper with then British Prime Minister Tony Blair and Bob Geldof who were both in Addis Ababa for a Commission for Africa (CFA) summit. Then *The Sun*'s Editor, Dominic Mohan, had come up with the idea of re-recording the Band Aid single 'Do They Know It's Christmas?' two decades after its original release. When I suggested it to Geldof, he batted straight back: *'Only if you fucking organize it.'*

The Sun subsequently flew Birhan to London for the recording in November 2004. Former Beatle Sir Paul McCartney, U2's Bono and Coldplay's Chris Martin either sang or played. Birhan's retelling of her heart-rending story as the symbol of Live Aid helped push the song to Number One in the British charts and raised £3 million for Africa. It was also a factor in pushing Geldof and others to organize the 'Greatest Show on Earth', the Live 8 concerts in 2005.

I was with Birhan and her friend and mentor Bisrat throughout the Band Aid re-recording and Live 8. They both became good friends. Birhan was born in a mud-walled hut into a subsistence-farming world that had changed little in millennia. The glitzy pop world was naturally an acute culture shock to her. With all the pride and dignity of her people, she remained wonderfully unaffected by all the razzmatazz. Slowly Birhan's confidence grew. Over time she began to confide the horrors of her early life and the joys that would later come. Our families met and became friends. In 2007 I took my mother, Sue, on holiday to Tigray to meet Birhan's family. My late mum, who owned a smallholding in Devon, spent hours discussing the finer points of cattle rearing with Woldu. In December 2009, Birhan asked me if I would write her life story for *The Sun*. When I suggested it would be better served as a book, she readily agreed. All author's profits will be split equally between Birhan and the charity that supported her, the African Children's Educational Trust (A-CET).

During the long hours of interviews and research in Ethiopia for this book, Birhan and her father Woldu have been incredibly generous with their time and hospitality. Both discussed family bereavements and harrowing events that they had sometimes not spoken about since the days of the famine. They always remained cheery and unfailing hosts. There was an endless stream of the world's best coffee and Woldu always made sure he sent me home with a huge pot of wonderful Tigrayan honey. I was also privileged enough to spend an Ethiopian Christmas Day at the family home. Birhan's stepmother, Letebirhan, and sisters, Lemlem and Silas, were also extremely patient and helpful when interviewed. Birhan's fiancé, Birhanu, was equally welcoming. They remain an amazingly close, extended African family, all completely unchanged by the global attention Birhan has received.

I found out much of the family's latter good fortune was down to the distinguished Canadian journalist Brian Stewart. His crew from the Canadian Broadcasting Corporation (CBC) had originally filmed Birhan when she was close to death. Brian was a reporter who didn't forget the horrors he witnessed when he reached the comforts of home. He later returned to Ethiopia and made sure Birhan and her siblings had schooling and the family a decent home. Brian's flurry of transatlantic emails for this book were astonishing in their detail and candour. Birhan's story is thus Brian's too. The family say they owe him everything and a large photograph of Brian has pride of place on Woldu's eucalyptus-wood chest of drawers. Brian's former CBC colleague Colin Dean, with him in Ethiopia in 1984, and CBC News Senior Political Correspondent Terry Milewski also provided valuable insight.

The day after I first interviewed Birhan in October 2004, I discovered through both Anthony and expat gossip in Addis that Bob Geldof was travelling in a remote part of western Ethiopia. Thumbing through the Lonely Planet guidebook I found the most likely hotel he would be staying in. The receptionist confirmed that they did indeed have a Mr Geldof staying there who was having a shower after a long day on the road. '*How the fuck did you find me?*' was Geldof's startled response when I got hold of him. I waited for him to use another expletive-ridden expression when asked for an interview. Instead, he proceeded to rattle through the Band Aid story, providing reams of headline-grabbing quotes, while barely drawing breath.

When Geldof and Birhan met for the first time just days later it was a special moment for both of them. Live Aid bound them together. Birhan's vitality and promise encapsulated everything that he had been banging his fist about for 20 years. And Africa keeps calling him back. Travelling in his adored Ethiopia, he is a force to be reckoned with – sometimes tearful at what he witnesses, at other times seething with rage at his inability to get things done quicker. He's never, ever sanctimonious and his knowledge of the aid business is now extraordinary. It has to be. The media is waiting, licking its lips, for him to slip up. Yet, I believe his mass-mobilization of public support for Africa will see him come to be recognized as one of the most significant public figures of the late 20th century.

Geldof called Birhan the 'Daughter of Live Aid' and Birhan loves him, she says, as another father. His wonderful foreword to this book is greatly appreciated.

Snappy-dressing, 30-something famine survivor Bisrat Mesfin and grey-haired former British Army officer David Stables are an unlikely double act, but together they run A-CET, a small charity that provides education for vulnerable Ethiopian children. The results are astonishing: graduates include a doctor, a human rights lawyer, a systems analyst and a human biologist. One A-CET pupil, Sammy Assefa, made it to Britain's Sangar Institute in Cambridge to carry out vital PhD research into mosquitoes to combat the scourge of malaria. Both Bisrat and David have been astonishing in their support since 2004. Bisrat was at Birhan's side throughout her journey, which culminated in Live 8. He provided the translation during interviews from Ethiopian languages Tigrinya and Amharic for this book. Although Birhan's

English is now reasonable, for many of our conversations she found it easier to speak in her native Tigrinya.

There is no literal translation from the Tigrinya and Amharic script to English. 'Mekele' can be spelt 'Mek'ele', 'Makele', 'Makale', 'Mekelle', and so on. I have tried in this book to use the most commonly used form or, for names, the spelling Birhan's own family prefers. Dates and times have been converted into their Western forms.

My Editors at *The Sun,* Rebekah Brooks, former Chief Executive of the paper's parent company News International, and Dominic Mohan, have been incredibly supportive. They have consistently commissioned me to write development features from Somalia to Sierra Leone and many nations in between.

The Sun's legendary Royal Photographer Arthur Edwards accompanied me to Ethiopia when I first met Birhan and was a constant source of shrewd journalistic advice and ready wit. He also provided some wonderful pictures for the book as did his son Paul, also a *Sun* photographer. My brother, Giles Harvey, also helped with processing pictures and my partner, Karen Lee, spent many hours transcribing interviews. I'd also like to thanks *Sun* colleague Sharon Hendry for introducing me to New Holland and my publisher Aruna Vasudevan for her insight and patience as deadlines loomed.

Birhan is desperately proud of her homeland and its unique culture. She wishes Ethiopia was known in the West for more than just famine. Today, she works tirelessly to end poverty and suffering in Ethiopia. Her mother, Alemetsehay, and sister, Azmera, died in the famines of the 1980s. Birhan would like to make sure they, and the countless others who perished in those dark days, are never forgotten.

–Oliver Harvey, Castle Hotel, Mekele, May 2011

PROLOGUE

BIRHAN WOLDU STARED with wonder at the teeming mass of humanity stretching as far as her eyes could see. From her position high in the wings of the huge Live 8 stage the people seemed all jumbled together on the cropped grass of Hyde Park. Just their little heads and raised, spindly limbs were showing. It made her think of the writhing nests of termites she had seen back home in Ethiopia. There was just enough breeze for flags to flutter in the muggy heat of a London summer's day – St George Crosses, Welsh dragons, a Red Hand of Ulster, several in the colours of the rainbow. Banners read: *'Wow Bob, it's huge'*, *'Hello World'* and *'Live 8 before it's too late'*. The words of the celebrated Indian human rights activist Mahatma Gandhi flashed up on giant video screens. *'First they ignore you, then they laugh at you, then they fight you, then you win.'* Outside the park, London's streets were largely empty. Most people were at home watching the 'Greatest Show on Earth' on TV. It was the topic of conversation in every pub and every taxi driver had his or her view.

Birhan surveyed the crowd with all the noble and proud bearing of her people who came from the mountains of Tigray Province. Her hair was styled in the traditional way. Plaited into neat cornrows on her crown, it flared out, luxuriantly bouncing on her shoulders. She wore a simple white tunic embroidered with small, light blue Christian crosses. Wrapped around the 24-year-old's shoulders was a bright white *shamma* linen shawl stitched here and there with red, blue and green diamonds. Her brown eyes sparkled with life; her clear skin was the rich colour of Ethiopian coffee. Like many from her region, she had a little scar etched on her forehead in the shape of a crucifix. She stood now, like an Ethiopian princess, on a 2 metre- (6.56 feet) wide platform by the side of the huge stage. Bundles of cables ran everywhere like creeping vines. Stacks of guitars stood on castors and a huge silver drum kit was being assembled by frantic roadies.

Just 48 hours earlier, Birhan had been in her family's stone-walled, corrugated iron-roofed cottage in the remote Ethiopian Highlands. Their cow was tethered to an olive tree outside and bantam chickens pecked the tinder-dry dark brown soil. When Birhan was younger she had slept on stiff ox skins in a dung-walled hut with a thatched roof in a lonely mountain valley. Alone with her goats on the high alpine meadows for the daylight hours, the crust of bread she brought from home often would not be enough to stave off hunger. She would lie down beneath the nanny goats' back legs and suckle warm milk straight from their teats.

London was a different world. The roaring traffic never seemed to stop and the red buses of the British capital were huge. Amazing food, more than Birhan could ever have imagined, piled high in front of her. After trying hamburgers for the first time, she had now eaten two in as many days. Then there were the people, rushing, always rushing. Why didn't they say 'hello' when they passed each other in the street? It would be rude to

walk past people in Tigray without greeting them first. She
was glad to have her friend from home, Bisrat Mesfin, with her
at this huge concert. She knew that her English wasn't always
good and Bisrat was much more confident when dealing with
the *farenjis* (foreigners). His girlfriend, Rahel Haile Selassie,
had also come along to keep them company.

All afternoon the wide-eyed Ethiopians had watched the
parade of rock stars trooping past in their lovely clothes. Bisrat
had pointed out an older *farenji* called 'Paul' whom he said had
once been in a band called The Beatles. Birhan had never heard
of him nor of his group. Earlier Paul (Sir Paul McCartney) had
played The Beatles' iconic song 'Sergeant Pepper's Lonely
Heart's Club Band' along with rock band U2. '*It was twenty
years ago today…*', they sang, setting the right note for the day.
As Paul squeezed past the throng of supermodels and film
stars, U2 released a cloud of 200 white doves which soared high
over the crowd as the band roared into its hit 'Beautiful Day'.

Singer Bono then paused, saying: 'This is our time. This is
our chance to stand up for what's right. We're not looking for
charity, we're looking for justice. We can't fix every problem,
but the ones we can fix, we must.'

The crowd seemed so happy; everyone was dancing. Birhan
was led to a green Portakabin where a pretty woman with dyed
red hair put blusher and eyeshadow on her face. It was the first
time she had ever worn make-up and she liked the way it
looked so much that she thought she must remember to take
some back to Ethiopia with her.

She didn't know much pop music, preferring the traditional
Arabian-tinged music of her homeland. Madonna was the only
name on the bill that Birhan recognized before arriving in
Britain. Birhan was awestruck.

Now, in a pale linen Nehru suit, his straggly hair tucked
under a baggy black cap, musician Bob Geldof came up and

hugged Birhan tight, before saying: 'Ok, darling, this is it. You'll be fine.' Standing in the stage wings, Geldof, his dark brown eyes aflame with emotion, seemed tense. Birhan smiled. She appeared as serene and calm as ever. Geldof swallowed hard.

To a deafening roar from the 205,000 crowd, Geldof strode to the centre of the vast Live 8 stage. The Father of both Band Aid and of Live Aid 20 years earlier had, it seemed, done the unthinkable again. It was July 2, 2005, and he had managed to focus the world's attention once again on the plight of Africa by amassing almost every leading musician who had picked up a guitar in the last 40 years. There stood Sir Paul, a re-formed Pink Floyd, The Who, U2, Sir Elton John, Madonna, Coldplay, Mariah Carey, Sting and George Michael. In 1985 the concerts had been held in London's Wembley Stadium and Philadelphia's John F. Kennedy Stadium. Today there were other Live 8s taking place in Toronto, Tokyo, Johannesburg, Paris, Rome, Berlin and Moscow, and once again, in Philadelphia. Then, with an estimated three billion eyes on him from every corner of the globe – and the G8 leaders of the world's richest and most powerful nations about to meet on British soil – Geldof stopped the music. He had something to say.

'Some of you were here 20 years ago. Some of you were not even born. I want to show you why we started this long, long walk to justice. It began … because many of us around the world watching here now saw something happening that was so grotesque in this world of plenty. We felt physically sick that anyone should die of want and decided we were going to change that. I want to show you, just in case you forgot, why we did this. Just watch this film.'

With a wave of his hand Geldof motioned to the massive video screen behind him. US band The Cars' haunting track 'Drive', with its melancholy keyboard refrain, echoed through the massive PA system. *'Who's gonna tell you when it's too late, who's gonna tell you things aren't so great...*' A stark film of Ethiopia's almost-biblical famine, when an estimated one million Tigrayan farmers perished of starvation, began to play. It was the same footage shot by a CBC news crew that had been shown at the original Live Aid concert two decades before.

An emaciated little boy, his legs mere bone and twitching sinew, kept trying to get to his feet in the early morning Tigray mist. Again and again. Then he slumped down, defeated. There was no strength left in his hunger-wracked body. Another skeletal boy stared blankly at the camera before burying his face in his bony hands. More and more children followed in a ghastly parade of the dead and dying. Then for a few moments the camera lingered on the tortured face of a little girl. Her desperate father had carried her to a clinic as she fought for life, but a nurse had told him it was hopeless. She gave the child just 15 minutes to live. The little girl's sunken brown eyes were lifeless behind half-closed lids. Her sallow parchment skin pulled taut against protruding cheekbones. Her swollen lips parted as she apparently took her last breath. Then the film stopped – the child's ghostly face in 10 metre- (32.8 feet) high freeze-frame above the now silent thousands.

At Live Aid on July 13, 1985, the same video had stopped the world. Twenty years later it had the same effect. TV cameras panning along the ranks of pop fans in their white 'Make Poverty History' wristbands picked up the unrestrained grief. Tears flowed and arms were flung around strangers. Now Geldof, his voice croaky with emotion, motioned up at the Ethiopian child's agonized face and spoke again.

'See this little girl – she had minutes to live 20 years ago. And because we did a concert in this city and Philadelphia, last week she did her agricultural exams at the school she goes to in the northern Ethiopian Highlands. She's here tonight this little girl. Birhan. Don't let them tell us that this doesn't work.'

Suddenly there she was on the Live 8 stage. She was alive.

Birhan, with Bisrat in her wake, walked over to Geldof and kissed him on the lips. Dignified and radiating an inner calm, the young woman's jubilant smile flashed around the globe by TV satellite in an instant. The thousands watching in Hyde Park were stunned into disbelieving silence. More tears were now wiped away. It seemed inconceivable that any of those children in that film, their bodies so grotesquely malformed by hunger, could have survived. The little girl who had come back from the dead took the microphone as billions watched on television on every continent and in every corner of Earth.

Slowly, in the rich tones of her native Tigrinya language, she said: 'Hello from Africa. We Africans love you very much. It's a great honour to be here and stand on the Live 8 stage. We love you very much. Thank you.' Bisrat translated her words into English as the crowd roared its approval.

They were a few simple words but enough to grab the world's attention. Her mere presence said more than a multitude of slogans and worthy speeches ever could. Birhan was living proof that aid worked. That the millions who had bought Band Aid's 'Do They Know It's Christmas?' charity record and who had thrown loose change into rattled tins and buckets hadn't done so in vain. Countless Birhans had been saved thanks to Live Aid and numerous other aid initiatives. This beautiful, intelligent woman was now brimming with potential, her dream to become a nurse, like those who gently cradled her as she lay close to death during Ethiopia's Great Famine of 1984.

From the giant Hyde Park PA system Geldof's voice boomed out once again: 'Don't let them tell you this stuff doesn't work. It works – you work – very well indeed.'

As he uttered the words 'from one immensely strong woman to another', Madonna bounded on stage. In a crisp figure-hugging white waistcoat and flowing white trousers, she sashayed over to Birhan and kissed her gently on the lips. The Queen of Pop, a diamond-encrusted 'M' dangling from her neck, was visibly overcome with emotion. Pausing momentarily to compose herself, her alabaster-white hand clasped Birhan's sinuous brown arm and raised it skywards. With that gesture the two women acknowledged the triumph of human spirit, the uniting of the First World and the Third.

Madonna carried on clutching Birhan's hand as she launched into her hit 'Like a Prayer'.

'Are you ready, London, to start a revolution? To change history?' Madonna demanded.

Bisrat, proudly wearing the T-shirt emblazoned with the name of the African Children's Educational Trust (A-CET) charity that he helps run, danced along, all the time feeling like this was a dream.

As Madonna started her second song, 'Ray of Light', Birhan and Bisrat walked back to where I was waiting for them in the stage wings; their elation shone brightly in their faces. Birhan was transfixed as she watched Madonna sing: *'Faster than the speeding light she's flying, trying to remember where it all began…'* Bisrat explained that this was a perfect song for his friend. *Birhan* meant 'light' in their language.

My newspaper, *The Sun,* had flown Birhan almost 6,000 km (3,700 miles) from Ethiopia for the concert. It had been a roller coaster 10 months since she and I had first met. What had started as an interview with Birhan at her Tigray home as part of a series on the 20th anniversary of Ethiopia's famine had mushroomed into something incredible.

There had been the emotional meeting with then British Prime Minister Tony Blair and Geldof in the Ethiopian capital Addis Ababa. This in turn led to the re-recording of the Band Aid single 'Do They Know It's Christmas?' The impetus from the song was a factor in pushing an initially unenthusiastic

Geldof to get behind a concert on the anniversary of Live Aid. Since then Birhan, Bisrat and I had become good friends.

As they emerged from the glare of billions, the relief was huge. We hugged in disbelief, our eyes prickling as the tears welled. When Birhan had enthusiastically agreed to appear at the concert she couldn't possibly have imagined the scale of the occasion. She said she wanted to do it because she knew what it was like to be starving hungry and didn't want other African children to suffer like she had done. Her composure and grace had been astonishing and humbling. Despite outward appearances, she admitted her heart had been fluttering as she waited backstage with all the pop stars. The devout Ethiopian Orthodox Christian had put herself in the hands of the Lord as she had throughout her tumultuous life. With the eyes of the world on her, she had found strength.

'I thought of the years of suffering my family and my country had endured,' Birhan explained. 'I wanted to show the world we Ethiopians are a proud and strong people. I wanted my father, Woldu, to be proud after all the sacrifices he had made for me.' Birhan explained that Woldu had always told her that God had spared them from the famine for a reason. 'I think today was the reason,' she said solemnly. An elated Geldof, hugging his partner, the French actress Jeanne Marine, added: 'Birhan's story is what this whole thing is about.'

If Live Aid was about charity then Live 8 was about justice, the organizers said. The brutal fact was that two decades on from Live Aid 50,000 people – 30,000 in Africa alone – were still dying each day from easily preventable diseases. It was true that Live Aid had raised over US $100 million – by far the most a charity has made in a single event – and had almost doubled that through subsequent sales and merchandizing. It was an astonishing achievement but it didn't solve Africa's woes. Band Aid had been a plaster but it didn't go to the root causes of what had kept Africa hungry and sick.

Geldof had subsequently immersed himself in development theory after Live Aid. He found the aid business was far from simple. He was staggered to learn that Live Aid's US $100 million was the amount poor nations had to pay back to Western nations in debt repayments every three or four days. For decades, poor countries spent more money repaying old debts than they did on health and education combined. Most of the billions had been accumulated under corrupt regimes during the Cold War and had accrued more and more interest. Trade rules and tariffs and taxes have also kept Africa poor. The apparently generous West was doing very well from the impoverished undeveloped world. A stark statistic quoted in 2005 was that for every US $1 given by rich nations in aid, US $2 was taken back in unfair trade.

The leaders of the G8 club of the wealthiest nations on Earth were due to meet at the luxury Scottish hotel Gleneagles in four days time. Geldof summed up Live 8 by saying that the world had spoken. He had a mandate and the political demands were 100 percent debt cancellation for the world's poorest nations, fairer trade laws and doubling the levels of aid to US $50 billion a year in return for better governance. He hoped that Birhan had shown the politicians how much the world lost every time a child dies.

The world's most powerful man had been watching the pop concert. US President George W. Bush later told Geldof in a private meeting: 'The most moving moment was when Birhan, the child who had appeared at death's door in a film at the Live Aid concert in 1985, came out.' Geldof was clear about the importance that Birhan's show-stealing appearance at Live 8 had on Bush. 'It clearly reminded him that when politicians negotiate in the rarefied atmosphere of a place like Gleneagles, there are individuals like her who live and die by their decisions.'

Now Birhan joined her friend Rahel to sip fruit cocktails in the backstage hospitality area at Live 8. Later she would allow herself a glass of red wine.

In the VIP zone free lobster and wine were served, but Birhan preferred her new favourite dish, a burger and chips. She had spent the earlier part of the day backstage, unknown and largely ignored by the great and the good. Now she was the centre of a social whirl.

Ex-Manchester United star David Beckham came over to greet Birhan, with his wife Victoria. They posed for pictures with her. Beckham looked positively delighted. 'I've heard about you Birhan and I think it's wonderful you are here today.' Bisrat, then a United fan, found it difficult to contain his glee. 'Thank you Mr David, sir.' A photograph of that time has pride of place in Bisrat's home in Mekele even though he has since switched his allegiance to Arsenal.

Then Hollywood star Brad Pitt came over. Bisrat had to explain to Birhan who the blond-haired *farenji* was. The actor told Birhan that she was 'a very special person'. Later she would comment that he had very kind eyes. Billionaire philanthropist Bill Gates and UN Secretary General Kofi Annan strolled past, as did Sir Paul McCartney with wife Heather Mills, capturing the day on a video recorder. They were no more recognizable to Birhan than the other *farenjis* in the crowd at the front of the stage.

Suddenly Birhan's eyes widened and she began giggling with excitement. She had finally recognized a face among the celebrity-studded crowd. It was Jeremy Clarkson, the comparatively less glamorous presenter of BBC motor show Top Gear. The programme is shown abroad on BBC World and is a favourite with Ethiopians. A large glass of rosé in hand, Clarkson was happy to pose for pictures. Later, Birhan, Bisrat and Rahel were back on the little 2 metre- (6.56 feet) wide gantry to watch The Who and a re-formed Pink Floyd play for the first time in over 20 years under the slogan: 'No More Excuses'.

Bear-like concert promoter Harvey Goldsmith, a giant wall clock dangling around his neck, barked orders out at the pop stars, who shuffled around backstage as if they were errant schoolchildren. Then, Sir Paul McCartney was back on stage to lead a mass singalong to The Beatles' hit 'Hey Jude' with the artists who had performed and the rapturous crowd.

Birhan stood swaying along to the music, smiling softly to herself as she watched transfixed. It had been a special day, one so different from her normal life.

Then it was over – Live 8 had pulled off what Live Aid had achieved 20 years before. Cynicism had been banished at least for one day, it seemed.

Leaving on foot through throngs of euphoric pop fans to head back to their Mayfair hotel, the three Ethiopians nattered away about what they had seen and heard. Some people in the crowd recognized Birhan. Politely smiling, most nodded 'hello' at her and kept walking. Others shook her hand with excitement.

The next morning over breakfast, Birhan was more talkative than usual. She had been unable to sleep in the strange, crisp white hotel sheets and had lain awake thinking of home. Of her beloved mountains of Tigray where that morning her father Woldu would wake with the rising sun to harness his lyre-horned plough oxen.

She loved the excitement of London, riding on the tube and seeing the people from all over the world – and the burgers, of course. She knew there were money and jobs here and good hospitals and great universities. But she wanted to go back home. Live 8 had helped Birhan understand her life, she explained to me. She now realized how the spirit of Live Aid had galvanized Western goodwill all those years ago and exactly what her part in it had meant. She finally understood why the *farenji* TV crews and reporters had wanted to talk to her.

Birhan had always found it difficult to speak about the famine days of the 1980s. She had been very young, it was true, but perhaps she had also blocked out the true horror of what had happened out of necessity. Her mother, Alemetsehay, and five-year-old sister, Azmera, had perished in the Great Hunger after all. Now Birhan began to talk as she hadn't been able to before. She told of how she'd wept as her father spoke of what she called the 'hunger time'; how the men with guns had come for their family and pushed them like cattle onto an old Russian plane, stealing them away to a resettlement camp in the Ethiopian Lowlands, around 1,300km (800 miles) away from their home. She spoke of how her father had told them that they would walk home, even though they were penniless and starving. That he would carry Birhan and her little sister on his shoulders all the way back to their ancestral mountains. To Tigray. To home.

She began to tell her family's story, of her father's struggle, of the epic journey to life.

INTO THE
DARKNESS

GARDEN
OF EDEN

THE MOUNTAINOUS NORTH of Ethiopia is a beautiful land long populated with farmers, priests and warriors. A rugged vastness, which had its first Christian king in the fourth century, the God-fearing people here believe the Lowlands are bedevilled by disease, strange people and savage beasts. Dotted with rock-hewn churches and lonely cliff-top monasteries, the mountain ramparts have repelled invaders for millennia.

It is here that Birhan Woldu came into this world mewling and kicking on a dried ox skin splayed across the sandy floor of a mud-walled hut known in the Tigrinya language as a *sekela*. It was an easy and relatively painless birth. Thankfully there were no complications for her mother, Alemetsehay, who soon cradled the wailing baby while a neighbour helped cut the umbilical cord with a sharp blade. If there had been a problem, mother and daughter would have been in the hands of the Almighty. The isolated hamlet of Lahama, with no electricity or running water, is on the high plateau of Tigray Province in Ethiopia's remote north. A trained doctor or midwife with even rudimentary knowledge of modern medicine were at best five hours away on foot across the desolate Highlands.

Birhan's father, Woldu Menamano, was out working his little terraced fields with his two sturdy plough oxen. As the red sun began to dip below the mountain crags, he made his way back through the lush fields of wheat, sorghum and barley, which swayed in the mountain breeze. Soon Woldu could see the rising plumes of white smoke billowing from Lahama's cluster of dung- and wicker-walled, thatched *sekelas*.

Before Woldu went inside, a white-robed priest blessed the baby, sprinkling holy water on Birhan and around the *sekela*, its beams and thatched straw roof turned charcoal-black with woodsmoke. Woldu paused for a moment to allow his eyes to adjust from the fading sunlight to darkness. Bending down, he slowly made the sign of the Christian Cross over the baby's forehead and whispered his own blessing. Tradition dictated he would not be able to hold his new daughter until she had been baptized, 80 days after her birth.

Woldu is a tiny man, barely 1.5 metres (5 feet) high, with a heavily lined, leathery face, a testament to a lifetime spent guiding the olive-wood plough and tending his cattle under the blazing African sun. Sipping *bune*, the rich Ethiopian coffee, or a home-brewed maize *tella* beer, he is a natural storyteller with a lyrical turn of phrase that often remains undiluted, even when translated from his native Tigrinya language. Birhan and the rest of Woldu's extended family all listen reverently when he speaks. Today, wearing a treasured, but threadbare pale cream suit, a traditional white *gabi* shawl draped over his shoulders, protection against the chill of the mountain night air, Woldu's dark eyes widen at the memory of Birhan's birth. He already had two girls, Lemlem, aged four, and Azmera, just two.

'I was so happy to set eyes on my beautiful little Birhan for the first time. My own childhood had been full of death, despair and suffering. I wanted my little girl to have a different life. I had passed the darkness of my early life and everything was now bright. So we called our new daughter *Birhan*, which means "light" in our language. Tigrayan farmers prefer boys; they are strong and can plough but I love my girls. I felt God had looked on me with fortune. I now had my own farm and a third daughter. The harvests had been good; I had honey and yoghurt for my beautiful wife and children.'

The little girl took her father's first name 'Woldu' as her surname, following Ethiopian custom. There was no birth certificate, no registration. Nor could anyone in the extended family read and write to record the event. Like many in Ethiopia's rural heartlands, Birhan does not know her birth date nor the exact year in which she was born. Woldu himself estimates that he is approximately 63. He laughs at what he sees as the Western fixation with age, saying: 'I know when the sun rises and falls. Is that not enough? We were more worried about getting through each harvest with enough food for our children than worrying how old we were. God decides how long you have in this world.'

The best guess for Birhan's birth year, her family say, is 1981 in the Western calendar. In January of that year former Hollywood actor Ronald Reagan became US President, just as the Cold War with the Soviet Union became more icy. In Britain, Prime Minister Margaret Thatcher was presiding over the yuppie age of materialism.

At some 2,300 metres (7,546 feet) above sea level, high in Tigray's burnt-brown mountains, the often harsh life in isolated Lahama had remained largely unchanged for its subsistence farmers since the time of Christ. On a rocky and sun-baked incline above a meandering river valley, 20 or so extended families lived in *sekela* huts. Their thatched conical roofs made them resemble a cluster of button mushrooms from a distance. Richer families lived in hand-quarried stone *hidmo* farmsteads of astonishingly skilled masonry. All were scattered above the banks of a river called Mai-Shashasta, meaning 'water splash', which is little more than a trickle for much of the year.

Birhan remembers the seasonal rains coming and turning it into a swirling, muddy torrent as flash floods swept the rich soil from the mountains. In the early morning and late afternoon she would accompany her sisters, Lemlem and Azmera, and the village children as they trekked laughing and singing down to the river bank in knots of threes and fours. With their clay pots, jerry cans and plastic bottles they would haul back all the water needed for their families' daily cooking and cleaning. Dangling from their necks by a thin cord given to them at baptism were lucky charms and talismans to ward off evil spirits, horrific diseases and times of hunger. 'There was so much laughter,' Birhan remembers. 'Life was so carefree at times. When the harvests were good, Lahama was like a paradise.'

Yet, when the rains fail in the Highlands, a common occurrence, there is drought, and if they keep failing, famine. In this precarious land the families are purposefully large, as security against the ravages of starvation and disease.

The mountains are often shrouded with mist as the sun rises. Temperatures sometimes drop well below freezing and the howling winds make it seem even colder. Birhan remembers the whole family huddling together at night to keep warm while they slept on ox skins under blankets. Then the midday sun could be broiling and unforgiving.

The rains were good when Birhan was a baby. Irrigated fields become lush green against the surrounding burnt hills. Woldu grew carrots, sorghum, spinach, barley, wheat and the native *tef* grain, the main ingredient of Ethiopia's staple dish *injera* bread. Another delicacy Birhan remembers the villagers loved was the prickly pear cactus fruit that grew throughout the village. Honey is also a delicacy – when the big *meher* rains come in mid-June, the flowers on the mountain pastures bloom in a burst of life, allowing bees to produce a distinct, sweet fluid famous throughout the country. Woldu says his hives produced some of the best honey in the village. Often served with crisp white bread as a church festival meal, it is also used to make *tej*, a honey wine that is the national drink of Ethiopia.

After the valley has blossomed, it is alive with bird life. Brilliant white cattle egrets bob up and down on the swirling air currents like giant butterflies above the river meadows. Carmine bee-eaters, with their brilliant green–blue head plumage and pinkish brown wings, feast on parasites while perched on the back of the cattle.

'Lahama was our Garden of Eden,' Birhan says, her face lighting up at the memory. 'The fields would turn bright green after the big rains. There was a little patch of grass sheltered by acacia trees where the children of the village came together to play. We called it *Maida-Tseba*. It was just a small patch of meadow and a few scattered bushes but it was magical to us. It was our secret world. Although it was a beautiful valley, life was very hard for my father who would work all the daylight hours in the fields. There were no schools or doctors in Lahama then. There was no electricity, TVs or radios. We had no idea what was going on in the outside world. I'm not sure we really cared.'

Woldu would rise with the sun and work the fields with his oxen, whose sweeping horns were identical to those seen painted on the walls of the tombs of Egypt's pharaohs. Like all rural Ethiopian men, he carried a hardwood staff called a *dula*. It is part weapon, walking stick and cattle prod. Most often it is used as a balance aid, laid across the shoulders with the owner's hands curled up to clasp the wood on either side. When the light begins to go in the late afternoon, the shadows cast by men carrying them in this way make them look as if they are being crucified. Some days Woldu would load his donkeys with firewood and honey to sell at the nearest market at Kwiha. The dustbowl town, a five-hour trek across ravines and upland pastures, is a natural gathering point for the cluster of mountain villages around Lahama. It lies on the main arterial trunk road connecting Addis Ababa, with the Tigrayan capital, Mekele, and, eventually, with neighbouring Eritrea and the Red Sea.

Alemetsehay, her hair painstakingly braided in traditional cornrows, would help out with the back-breaking harvesting and planting in the fields. Amid the swirling woodsmoke inside the *sekela*, Alemetsehay, a pewter Christian Cross dangling from her neck, would also spend much of her time preparing family meals. A daily chore was baking the spongy, pancake-like *injera* on a large, black, clay plate called a *mogogo* over a cow dung-fuelled fire. With Birhan, Lemlem and Azmera playing at her feet, she would grind grain, roast coffee beans and brew *tella* beer. The barefoot village children, their heads shaved bar a single long tuft (to enable God to pluck them to heaven should they fall sick), tended the goat and cattle herds, protecting them from attacks by hyenas. Later, when she was old enough, Birhan would become a goatherd, spending long days alone with her flock on the mountainside. But at that time, Lemlem and Azmera would drag along baby Birhan to Woldu's well-tended fields where they were charged with protecting the root crops from scavenging porcupines. 'If you want to kill them you have to hit their feet first with sticks or stones,' Woldu explains. 'Their feet are their weak points.'

Ethiopia is a land where elders and grey hairs are respected and obeyed. Birhan refers to her father as 'Ato Woldu' – 'Mr Woldu' – as a mark of respect. She listens intently as he describes his family's early years, a glass of *tella* beer in his hand. 'I love him so much. I owe every thing to him,' she says.

38

Devoutly Christian, Woldu tells how famine, pestilence and even plagues of locusts have dogged his six decades. The family patriarch was born in a *sekela* hut a six-hour walk over the mountains from Lahama in the village of Adi Hidug. The year, he thinks, was 1948. By the age of five he was orphaned – his father, Gebregergis, had perished from some undefined 'fever' (a description applied to most diseases in the mountains) and his mother, Aleme, died in childbirth, a still tragically common cause of death in this isolated region today. She was, Woldu says, 'light skinned' and so beautiful that 'people from other villages would call in just to gaze at her'. Woldu has a sharp memory and feels obvious pride in describing his family history in the Ethiopian oral tradition.

'We were a poor farming family. Life was very hard. Famine was not so bad then but we had plagues of locusts that made the sky go black. If the land grew infertile or there was famine we simply moved to another place where there was rain and good soil. There was plenty of space for us all then. There was no outside aid in those times. If you went hungry you died. We weren't educated people. School was nothing but a dream to me. I can't read or write. If you bought me a big clock and put it on the wall there I would have no idea what the time was. I just look at the sun and where it is in the sky. I only remember the time of year by the church feast days.'

Woldu was left in the care of his sisters. The family had 10 cows and many goats and Woldu was in charge of the livestock herds. He says his sisters treated him badly.

'My sisters' boys wouldn't go into the fields so I did all the work. I was always hungry. I would only be given a handful of roasted barley a day to eat. I was so unhappy I cried in the fields; then I cried silent tears when I slept in our *sekela*.'

At the age of 12 he ran away from home to work as a cattle herder for a rich family. In return the family gave him a patch of land to farm for himself. Any profits he made, he could keep. He had no home of his own and would sleep under the stars next to the cattle.

'I grew wheat. If I had a good crop I would lend 100kg (220lb) of the crop to those in need. When they could give it back they would give me 150kg (330lb). It was a sort of loan with interest. In the good times I would make a little money and I could buy clothes. If there were locusts I made nothing. I lived like this for many, many years during the Haile Selassie regime.'

Haile Selassie, Ethiopia's *Negus Negast* or 'King of Kings', was said to have a divine right to rule. The Ethiopian Constitution insisted he was the 237th monarch in an unbroken line from the biblical King Solomon and the Queen of Sheba. Other official titles bestowed on him were 'Elect of God' and 'Conquering Lion of Judah'. A tiny, seemingly mild-mannered man, Haile Selassie had ruled the nation since 1916, first as a regent, then from 1930 as Emperor. His lavish coronation seemed to confirm the biblical prophesy: *'Kings will come out of Africa.'* Jamaicans used his name before he assumed the crown, Ras Tafari Makonnen, to found a new faith they called 'Rastafarianism'. Haile Selassie, which means 'power of the trinity' in Amharic, was adopted as a living god, Jah, and marijuana as a sacrament. When the Emperor made a three-day visit to Jamaica in 1966, some people there were convinced miracles occurred, much to the bemusement of many Ethiopians. Groups of Rastafarians, encouraged by the Back to Africa movement, even migrated to Ethiopia and the town Shashemene, south of Addis Ababa, became their unofficial capital.

In his early years, Haile Selassie had made considerable efforts to modernize Ethiopia. Slavery had been abolished, schools, hospitals and roads constructed and he authorized the establishment of a parliament. But Ethiopia remained a feudal society in which the Emperor, aristocratic families and the

Church owned and controlled much of the land. Birhan points out that women were second-class citizens. They were not allowed to eat their main meals until their husbands were at the table. Around three-quarters of Ethiopia's peasant farmers were also tenants and Woldu remembers the Haile Selassie years as a time of endemic corruption to the cost of the peasants.

In the 1930s, however, Haile Selassie was hailed in the West, after his nation's stand against Benito Mussolini, Italy's fascist dictator. Mussolini, envious of the British and French African colonies, wanted to build an East African empire and he was desperate to avenge Italy's crushing defeat by an Ethiopian army at the Battle of Adwa in 1896. Like most Ethiopians, Birhan is very proud of her nation's stand against European colonialism. Italy had been humiliated at Adwa in northern Tigray when its army of 17,000 soldiers advanced into the Ethiopian Highlands but was routed by Emperor Menelik II's forces. The victory, Birhan explains, is seared into the national consciousness. It only added to the Ethiopians' belief that they were a special people.

In 1935 Mussolini stood before his supporters in Rome's Piazza Venezia and bellowed: 'We have patient for 40 years. Now we want our place in the sun.' Half-a-million Italian troops poured into Ethiopia using aerial bombardment and banned poison mustard gas in the advance. After a seven-month campaign, Addis Ababa was captured and Haile Selassie fled into exile, choosing the genteel English city of Bath as his new home. But while Ethiopia may have been occupied by the Italians, it was never successfully colonized. The mountains protected the people, just as they had before against waves of invaders throughout history. Birhan believes this independence has contributed to Ethiopia's evident confidence and self-esteem in the modern world.

In 1941, just five years after Mussolini's troops had arrived, Haile Selassie slipped across the border from Sudan back into his homeland. With the help of the British-led forces already confronting the Italians, the standard of the 'Lion of Judah' was raised once more. The old order resumed, the Emperor took possession of his palaces and the grinding, poverty-blighted life of millions of rural peasants remained unchanged. Under the 1967 Civil Code of Ethiopia, tenants had to pay 75 percent of their produce to their landlord, provide free firewood, free labour on the landlord's farm and free work as servants, cooks and guards at the landlord's home. Peasants faced constant fear of eviction. 'There was a lot of corruption under Haile Selassie. He may have been an honest man but he was not a good leader,' is Woldu's summation of that time.

In 1969, with the Emperor's 40th anniversary approaching, Woldu finally got his own farm. He had to apply to the local elders in Lahama for land and built his own *sekela* hut. He worked the land until his hands were rough and calloused. He harvested wild plants in the mountains and ploughed four different fields. Eventually, he managed to save up to buy a cow, goats and a donkey. Woldu explains that they are the basic domestic animals that every farmer needs to survive. After a year he had enough saved to buy another ox. 'I was in my early 20s; I felt fit and healthy and was ready to be with a woman.' He met Alemetsehay Berhe, who was working at a neighbouring farm.

'She was a hard worker and extremely beautiful,' Woldu recalls, smiling. 'She was trusting, calm and quiet. We didn't get married; there was no church service, nothing. We couldn't afford any celebration. We relied on trust and our belief in God. She helped work the fields with me, weeding. It was hard and dirty work but Alemetsehay never complained. We were just pleased to get through each season with enough to eat.'

In 1973, though, famine devastated Wollo Province next door to Tigray. Estimates of those that died vary between

40,000 and 200,000. In Lahama's winding river valley, Woldu and Alemetsehay managed to withstand the hardships brought on by the failed rains.

'There was a bad drought, a terrible time, but it wasn't everywhere,' Woldu remembers. 'If you had money there was still food in the markets. I was fine, I had made sure I had stored grain and had enough animals to get me through.'

The imperial government knew of the disaster unravelling in the north of Ethiopia but did little to help the peasants dying in their tens of thousands. To spare its reputation, Ethiopia also failed to seek international aid. British ITV correspondent Jonathan Dimbleby alerted the outside world to the catastrophe in Wollo. His raw documentary *The Unknown Famine* showed graphic scenes of the wasted cadavers of children who had starved to death. The impact in Britain was enormous, resulting in a public appeal that raised £6 million.

In early 1974 Haile Selassie's reign began to unravel. Units of the armed forces mutinied and there were student demonstrations and strikes by teachers and taxi drivers. There were also suggestions that Haile Selassie, then in his early 80s, was losing his faculties. US lawyer and historian Dr John Spencer, who had advised Ethiopia on international legal matters for decades, visited the ageing monarch that year. He says: 'It became apparent to me... that Haile Selassie was already retreating into a dream world. I withdrew with the piercing realization that the curtain of senility had dropped.'

In September 1974, a group of Marxist army officers became determined to overthrow the Emperor. Known as the Derg (meaning 'committee' in Ethiopia's ancient language Ge'ez), the cadre of revolutionaries showed Dimbleby's film, re-titled *The Hidden Hunger,* on Ethiopian national TV. Scenes of starving peasants were intercut with shots of Haile Selassie and his entourage sipping champagne, eating caviar and of the

43

Emperor feeding meat to his dogs from a silver tray. It was the end for the Lion of Judah. Bundled into the back seat of a green Volkswagen Beetle in his palace driveway by rebel army officers, he was never seen alive in public again. The 'King of Kings' would die a prisoner on August 27, 1975, the cause, according to Derg officials, 'respiratory failure' following complications from a prostate operation. His followers, however, insist the 3,000-year-old Solomonic dynasty ended when the Emperor was smothered with a wet pillow. His remains were buried under a lavatory in the palace grounds, only to be discovered 16 years later.

The Derg was led by Colonel Mengistu Haile Mariam, who soon developed a bloodthirsty lust for absolute power. Former BBC news correspondent Michael Buerk, who would famously alert the world to Ethiopia's 1984 famine, described him vividly as 'an outstandingly evil bastard, even for a continent stiff with vicious dictators'.

High in Tigray's secluded mountains the farming families of Lahama were anxious about what the fall of the Emperor would mean. 'When the king of bees dies you worry what will happen to the rest of the hive,' Woldu comments. 'We worried after the Emperor went. We were scared there would be chaos and anarchy. We had no TV, radio or telephones. We had to rely on what people told us about the Derg. In the beginning Mengistu was a good man. He wanted equality and said he would cut out corruption. But then the terrible Red Terror came. Life was cheap. People were killed for no reason.'

The Derg revolution was followed by the mass murder of sympathizers of the previous regime and of university students. One hundred thousand people are said to have been butchered in the Red Terror. Their bodies were left littering the streets of Addis Ababa on the orders of Mengistu. To lie unburied in such a religious country is a terrible humiliation for the relatives of the dead. When family members came out at night to bury their loved ones, Derg soldiers were waiting for them. They hung the bereaved from lamp posts as a warning to others of what might come.

Mengistu attempted to force the teachings of Marx and Lenin, as well as the purges and forced resettlements of Soviet Communist leader Joseph Stalin, on an African subsistence-farming people whose first allegiance was to the extended family, then to the church or mosque. The Derg also nationalized banks, industry and rural land. Turmoil and bloodshed swept the country as revolution raged.

In the mountains of Tigray, a guerilla force, the Tigrayan People's Liberation Front (TPLF), was formed, advocating independence for the province. (Ethiopia's present-day Prime Minister Meles Zenawi became its Chairman in 1985.) Bitter fighting between the TPLF and the government went on for years. Birhan's face contorts at the mention of the Derg. The men with guns even came to the remote, wind-blown valleys around Lahama. 'We tried to avoid the soldiers,' Woldu recalls. 'If the Derg soldiers wanted food we had to hand it over. It was a terrifying time.'

The rains had returned to the Highlands after the famine of 1973 and the harvests were plentiful in Lahama. Woldu and Alemetsehay decided to start a family and in about 1977 Lemlem, meaning 'green' or 'fertile', was born. Scratching his grizzled beard, Woldu says: 'Alemetsehay prepared me a lunch of *injera*, then less than an hour later Lemlem was born. She was a lovely child, very sweet natured.' Another girl, Azmera, followed in 1979 and two years later Alemetsehay was expecting again. This time with Birhan.

'Lemlem and Azmera were very similar children,' Woldu murmurs. 'Both were quiet, placid and very contented. Birhan was different from her older sisters. She was the most quick witted. Unlike her sisters, Birhan never stopped talking.'

45

However, when she was just one year old, Birhan was struck down by a mystery fever. Woldu and Alemetsehay prayed to the Lord. When their daughter grew weak, her eyes swollen, the local traditional healers knew exactly what had to be done. Woldu took a razor blade and carefully made several vertical incisions on the arches of Birhan's eyebrows. The 'bad' crimson blood flowed freely. Then using the blade again, he made another cut on her forehead, first a horizontal followed by a longer vertical incision that bisected the first. Slowly he intoned: *'In the name of the Father, the Son and the Holy Spirit'*. The bad blood flowed again. Like many in Ethiopia, Birhan has the mark of Christ, a crucifix-shaped scar now on her forehead.

Christianity is fundamental to Birhan's Highland people. The Ethiopian Orthodox religion arrived in these wild uplands some three centuries after Christ's death when Rome was still officially pagan and much of northern Europe was still centuries away from converting. There are 30 Old Testament references to Ethiopia or 'Cush' as it was known to the Hebrews. Moses himself married an Ethiopian woman. In Genesis it is written that the Ghion River, believed to be the Blue Nile, which has its source in Lake Tana in the Highlands, 'compasseth the whole land of Ethiopia'. The land is dotted with monasteries and holy relics. Should they stray from the path of righteousness, the God of the peasant farmers of Lahama is the vengeful and unforgiving Old Testament divinity of Abraham and Moses.

'The Church has always been central to our lives,' Birhan explains. 'We follow the calendar by feast days. Every day of the month is dedicated to a particular saint. My father remembers our family history by the feast days.'

The Orthodox Church services are in Ge'ez, an ancient Semitic language related to Hebrew and Arabic, which is sub-Saharan Africa's only ancient written language. It is the Latin of Africa, a liturgical language no longer spoken yet closely related to Ethiopia's national language Amharic, as well as Tigrinya. The Ethiopian Church claims a fragment of the True Cross is buried under the Gishen Mariam monastery in the Wollo region. In the holy city of Lalibela a solid gold cross is said to have miraculously appeared as a mason chiselled the walls of one of the city's famous rock-hewn churches. Legend has it that the holes in the stone surrounding Lalibela's Bet Giyorgis Church are the hoof prints left by St George mounted on a horse. Birhan has never been to Lalibela but it is her long-held dream to make a pilgrimage there.

In Aksum, north of Mekele, Ethiopia's greatest treasure, the biblical Ark of the Covenant, the wooden chest containing the stone tablets on which the Ten Commandments were inscribed, is said to lie in the treasury of the Church of Our Lady of Zion. However, only a single monk is allowed to see it. Replicas of the Ark, known as *tabots*, are kept in Lahama's Kidane Mehret Church and in every church across Ethiopia.

Like most Ethiopians, Birhan is convinced the Ark lies in her homeland. Woldu shares her faith. 'God has the power to make the sun rise every morning. Why shouldn't the Ark be in Aksum?' Many historians remain unconvinced, however.

Christianity arrived in Ethiopia in the fourth century spread by a Syrian monk called Frumentius. It is a story well known to Ethiopian schoolchildren. Captured as a boy when his ship docked on the Red Sea coast in what is now Eritrea, Frumentius was taken to the ancient city state of Aksum as a slave. The city in Tigray's Highlands was one of the powers of the ancient world. At its height it ruled a kingdom from the Nile in Sudan, across the Red Sea to Yemen. The third-century writer Manni described Aksum as one of the four great kingdoms in the world along with Rome, China and Persia. Frumentius rose to a position of power and eventually converted Aksum's King Ezana to Christianity, after which he became Ethiopia's first bishop. Today, Ethiopians know Frumentius as *Abba Selama, Kesaté Birhan* in Amharic – which translates as 'Father of Peace, Revealer of Light'.

Although Tigray is predominately Christian, Islam arrived in Ethiopia during the lifetime of the Prophet Muhammad. Some of his most respected disciples found refuge in Aksum, leading Muhammad to command his followers to 'leave the Abyssinians in peace'. Later the conquering armies of Islam swept through North Africa leaving Ethiopia cut off from the holy city of Jerusalem and the rest of Christendom. The word of the Prophet also spread down Africa's east coast on the dhows (one- or two-masted, lateen-rigged ships) of Arab traders. To the west and south, the country was surrounded by deserts and fierce Lowland tribes. A marooned outpost of Christianity, it led to the belief that it was the kingdom of the mythical medieval priest–king Prester John, a realm whose wealth and vast armies would one day come to the aid of its Christian brothers in the north. Birhan explains that Ethiopian Christians and Muslims today live happily side by side. They respect each other's faiths. Thus, Birhan's early life in Lahama revolved around the Church and her parents' little farm, a pre-industrial society that has changed little since the time of Christ.

'I gradually built up my herds,' her father says. 'Having cattle means prestige and wealth – the same as having many children. From cows you get milk and butter and then money. Then life is good. God had looked kindly on me. My family were all healthy; my herds strong.' At this point, Woldu pauses, remaining quiet for what seemed an age. The only sound was the twitter of weaver birds in a nearby acacia tree. His face suddenly contorts; his brown eyes far away as if seeing another landscape. 'Then our world turned black,' he murmurs. 'As pitch black as the darkest night.'

THE LAND
AND THE
SKY COLLIDE

THE ONCE TORRENTIAL mountain river of Mai-
Shahshahta running through Lahama's carefully tended,
terraced fields at first became a trickle. Its bed of pebbles and
clay became baked and cracked under the blast-furnace sun.
The solemn prayers at Kidane Mehret Church went
unanswered. The rains didn't come. First the *tef*, the wheat and
the barley failed to germinate in the dusty soil. Then the once
verdant pastures and scrub withered and died. Woldu and
the other mountain farmers were accustomed to regular
drought. They were prepared for such imminent disaster, for
God's wrath and in the good times Woldu built up reserves of
food and livestock. Excess grain was stored in huge woven
wicker barrels covered inside and out with cow dung to keep
the rats out. His herds of cattle and goats were large. He also
cultivated trade links with relatives and friends in other less
affected regions.

Woldu coped well with the first drought of 1982 when
Birhan was still being breastfed. He had reserves of both grain

and livestock. The children barely noticed the hardships and the family was still strong and together.

'Lemlem, Azmera and little Birhan, of course, had no idea of the approaching hard times,' says grey-bearded Woldu, sipping his first dark and sweet *bune* of the day. 'There was laughter around our *sekela*. We still had our goats and oxen and even honey. Alemetsehay was a wonderful mother. You could see the joy her children gave her in her eyes and her smile.'

When the rains failed for a second year, however, the russet, parched grassland shrivelled up and died in the relentless heat. Everything turned to dust. Woldu's herds had to travel further and further to find grazing from the hardier shrubs that could survive the drought. In the midst of this, Alemetsehay had news for Woldu. They would soon have another mouth to feed.

'I was blessed again with another daughter, little Silas,' Woldu says proudly. 'She was beautiful like my other girls. I promised to work harder so that we would all have enough to eat. I prayed to the Lord, but still the rains didn't come.'

As 1983 rolled into 1984, Woldu again prepared his land for the rainy season, but the rich mountain earth crumbled to a fine, dry powder as the olive wood plough sliced through it. The biting wind then whipped up the fertile topsoil and blew it far away from the Highlands. Satellite photographs from that year show a huge brown cloud drifting out from the Horn of Africa into the Indian Ocean. Once the scorched mountains had been covered by lush forest, but in 1984 just four percent of Ethiopia was tree covered. That meant more erosion and more rich topsoil blowing to the four winds. Woldu and the other farming families were soon digging into their reserve grain stores as the drought intensified. As vegetation died off the cattle were becoming weak.

'When the famine had started three years earlier it was okay, I was managing,' Woldu insists. 'I had two cows, two ploughing oxen and many goats. I had grain stores for when the bad times came. The drought was severe, but I was prepared. There were food stores further south in Tigray that we were able to buy. So, I sold the two oxen and a cow and many of my goats to get money for food. Then famine hit further south, too.'

The farmers in the bleak Highlands are used to living on the margins of survival. A religious work, the Ethiopian *Synaxarium,* records famine in the ninth century and reveals how 'great tribulation' had 'come upon our land, and all our men are dying of the plague, and our beasts and cattle have perished, and God hath restrained the heavens so that they cannot rain upon our land'. The leading Ethiopian historian Richard Pankhurst also records at least one famine a decade between the 15th and 19th centuries. The *Qefu Kan,* or 'Evil Days' (1888–92) killed as many as one-third of Ethiopians and is still seared into their folk memory. Locusts laid waste grain crops, rinderpest (a contagious viral disease) decimated cattle herds – and then the rains failed. Devastating famines in 1958, 1966 and 1973 saw tens of thousands starve to death. Now, it seemed, the Evil Days had returned for Birhan's family and the God-fearing people of Lahama. And yet, it wasn't just the elements conspiring against the villagers, this time the hunger was being exacerbated by man.

The Derg's brutal dictator Colonel Mengistu Haile Mariam had unleashed his troops in the Highlands to suppress rebellions against his rule. The man referred to by some as the 'Black Stalin' believed rebel groups like the TPLF were being nurtured by the civilian population. Thus, he used hunger as a weapon of war, turning a rural disaster into a catastrophe. Scorched earth tactics were employed: crops and pastures were torched, livestock stolen or killed and untold numbers of farmers displaced. Government forces also requisitioned food and rather than aiding peasant farmers, Mengistu diverted resources into promoting state farms. He was, to all intents and purposes, starving his own people. His brutal forces penetrated the remote mountains, windswept plateaus and plunging ravines around Lahama.

Woldu faced being robbed at the barrel of an AK-47 when he drove his donkeys, laden with grain and honey, across the mountains to Kwiha market. 'We couldn't take our short cuts to market anymore because the military were there. The Derg soldiers would check the grain in the sacks strapped on our donkeys by jabbing knives into the bags. We were terrified. In the daytime these Derg men were soldiers but at night the same people became *shiftas* (bandits), who stole our money, milk and food. If a woman was beautiful they would first tie up her husband and then rape her. It was a truly horrible and frightening time.'

Mengistu was well aware of the impending devastation in the north. Dawit Wolde Giorgis, head of the government's Relief and Rehabilitation Commission (RRC) and a member of Mengistu's central committee, had toured Tigray and Wollo in the summer of 1983. He saw thousands of hungry peasants crowded into relief camps. Returning, he sought a private audience with Mengistu, informing him that there were the 'makings of a terrible famine' if the rains failed again. His words as an Ethiopian contemporary eyewitness, indeed one from inside the regime, are worth dwelling upon.

As Dawit recorded in his memoirs *Red Tears*, he approached Mengistu and explained that they needed more money to deal with the crisis. He was told not to panic. Mengistu said, 'Don't let these petty human problems that always exist in transition periods consume you. There was famine in Ethiopia for years before we took power – it was the way nature kept the balance. Today we are interfering with that natural mechanism of balance, and that is why our population has soared to over 40 million.' Mengistu didn't elaborate further on this, but Dawit understood what he meant: 'Let nature take its toll – just don't let it out in the open. We need a façade for the outside world, so make it look like we're doing something.'

In February 1984, Dawit's RRC recorded 10,000 people dying in shelters each week. In March that figure had risen to 16,000. Driving on the main highway from Addis Ababa north to Wollo and Tigray, Dawit witnessed village after village facing devastation. The great spinal artery, which eventually leads all the way to the Red Sea, was clogged with masses of exhausted and starving people. Dignified mountain people, just like Birhan's family, had been forced to sell their herds, farming tools, household goods and jewellery for food. Then, in a final flight to try and save their lives, they made for the great trunk road from where any relief might come. Motoring to Korem on the Highland escarpment, Dawit found the town of 7,000 had been swamped by 100,000 desperate people who were gathered at a Save the Children relief shelter.

He witnessed 'the terrible agony of people forced to choose between leaving their dying wives, husbands or children behind, or staying to die with them... There were corpses everywhere, lined up in rows of ragged sackcloth shrouds or still uncovered in the midst of the crowd... Some bodies twitched helplessly, some writhed in agony as hunger ate away their living tissue... It was like walking through an open graveyard.'

Birhan was shocked years later when she found out that people in the United States and western Europe had too much to eat that year. The 1984 harvests there had been the biggest on record. In Britain it beat the previous record by more than 4 million tonnes (3.95 million tons). There were food mountains made up of the surplus stock. Mass starvation anywhere on the globe should simply have been impossible.

In April 1984, Dawit toured North America and Europe and addressed the United Nations (UN) requesting support. He told UN delegates that a 'severe drought of unprecedented magnitude' was ravaging his nation. He added: 'Starvation is currently the lot of over 5 million of our population.' Although Dawit estimated 900,000 tonnes (885,000 tons) of emergency grain would be needed for that year alone, realizing that it didn't have the means to distribute such a huge quantity, Ethiopia instead asked the international community for half that amount. The UN's Food and Agriculture Organization (FAO) placed the figure needed at 125,000 tonnes (123,000 tons). By August 1984, only 100,000 tonnes (98,420 tons) had been promised, much of it remaining undelivered.

In Ethiopia, Mengistu was livid at Dawit's intervention and what he saw as his cap-in-hand trip to the West. When Dawit went to his office, he was accused of exaggerating the problem and of having shown Ethiopia in a bad light. Mengistu would not listen to anything Dawit said, repeating again and again that this was just an 'ordinary food shortage' that was being used as a ploy. Finally, he ordered Dawit to stay put and not go on any more fund-raising tours abroad. He told him to do what he could to manage the situation without attracting any more attention.

While his people starved, Mengistu preferred lavishing Ethiopia's meagre funds on bullets and guns. More than half of the country's budget went on maintaining the despot's 300,000-strong army. The West, in the midst of the Cold War, was deeply mistrustful of the Marxist leader who seemed in no hurry to deal with the humanitarian crisis in his country. Both governments and relief agencies were also reluctant to prop up Mengistu's regime by providing aid for the hungry, which might instead enable him to concentrate his resources on fighting wars. As Oxfam official Tony Vaux puts it: 'Agencies were tired of helping a government that seemed to do little to help itself.'

Journalists were denied access by the regime to the famine-hit regions. The world was deprived of eyewitness reports of the unfolding catastrophe. The big *meher* rains that summer of 1984 tragically failed in Lahama and across a wide swathe of the north. Millions were now starving.

Mengistu deemed this a good time for a celebration. He decided that no expense would be spared for the lavish festivities marking the 10th anniversary of the revolution that removed Haile Selassie from power. At his headquarters, amid the splendour of Emperor Menelik's old palace in Addis Ababa, Mengistu oversaw plans for a huge new convention centre – the Great Hall of the People – that would seat 3,500 delegates from communist parties around the world.

Dressed in Soviet-cut military jacket and cap, he poured over details of the sumptuous festivities that would include troop marches, banquets and dancing. The price tag for the opulence planned was said to be as much as US $200 million. On September 12, 1984, Revolution Day, the procession of Soviet military hardware and goose-stepping troops snaked for 5 km (3 miles), beneath triumphal arches boasting slogans like, '*Long Live Proletarian Internationalism*'. Mengistu made a torturous five-hour speech. Some 800km (500 miles) north in Lahama, Birhan and her family were going hungry – like millions of peasants in his Communist utopia.

That summer Woldu looked to the skies for the *meher* rains, but the sun kept on blazing down and no showers came.

'There was no grass; the cattle started to weaken and fall ill. If you were strong enough you could walk far into the mountains and cut thorn branches for the cows but it was such hard work. We were now starving and weak.

'There was no food. Our animals started dying one by one.'

The piously Christian villagers were convinced that they had somehow brought God's vengeance upon themselves. That the rains failed because they had sinned. Woldu admits: 'God was angry with us. He has his time for being generous and a time for punishment. The hunger times were His punishment. What else could it be? Perhaps people hadn't been going to church or fasting properly.'

Birhan has heard the story of the Evil Days many times from her father. 'Ato Woldu was a very successful farmer who worked long years to build up his herds and provide for his family. He was a rich man; he had many cattle. It would have devastated him when they died. So, when the great hunger came it hit him hard. He was a proud man who valued being able to feed his children. He seemed to be able go anywhere and come up with something to eat. When the rains failed our paradise in Lahama had become a hell.'

There was little to eat but a few grains of corn. Alemetsehay would desperately eke out the food, dividing it carefully among the whole family. Soon she fell ill with a 'fever' becoming sallow skinned and weak. Alemetsehay's friend and neighbour, Letebirhan Tesfay came around to babysit the children for Woldu. 'I had to make sure the children were being looked after properly while I was in the fields looking for food or at the market,' Woldu recalls. 'I was so worried about Alemetsehay. We had no idea what the sickness was and there were no doctors in the village.'

As Alemetsehay grew more weak, she was unable to breastfeed little Silas. The baby's hungry screams filled the *sekela*. Birhan, Lemlem and Azmera wept too.

Letebirhan, her hair neatly plaited into cornrows in the traditional Tigrayan way, recalls: 'I let Silas suck my breast to comfort her and stop her tears. Then I fed her cow's milk. I was so worried for Alemetsehay. She fell weak bit by bit during the hunger times. We all had very little to eat, just a few handfuls of barley a day for the whole family. Alemetsehay was my great friend, a very beautiful, strong and tough woman. I was sure she would survive, she was fighting… for her daughters.'

Two weeks after his wife had fallen ill, Woldu had spent the day desperately trying to find fodder for his dwindling herds. When he came in from the fields, Alemetsehay's breathing was deep and rasping. After a while she fell silent and there was no breathing at all. With tears flooding his eyes, he blessed her and went outside to pray. Her young family wracked with grief, Alemetsehay was laid to rest close to the Kidane Mehret Church.

Birhan, who was around three years old, and baby Silas were too young to remember the tragedy. There were no pictures of Alemetsehay, no possessions, nothing to remember her by. Letebirhan increasingly took on responsibility for the family and Birhan grew up believing her to be her natural mother. Lemlem and Azmera would have known differently, but the truth remained unspoken.

'I can't remember my own mother,' Birhan says tearfully. 'That breaks my heart. The famine had taken her – like it took so many others. When I was in my 20s… I asked Letebirhan if she was my biological mother. She told me the truth immediately. We both broke down and wept. We hugged tightly for a long time. I love her so much. She has always been a wonderful mother to us all. The fact that my father didn't tell me Letebirhan was not my real mum is normal here in Ethiopia. If you adopt a child here you don't tell people. I don't blame anyone. There was so much tragedy in the famine times that people had to get on with their lives as best they could.'

Extended family and close friends are Africa's social security network. Letebirhan explains: 'When Alemetsehay fell ill she said to me: "Please look after the children if anything happens to me". It was a big responsibility. I felt I had to fulfil my promise to my friend and to help her lovely children. I raised them as my own. Birhan was lovely natured child... Lemlem and Azmera were quieter.'

Letebirhan was born in around 1960 in a mud-walled Lahama *sekela* across a rocky track from Birhan's family home when the valley was 'bright green'. She had been Alemetsehay's great friend. For over a year after her death, Letebirhan and Woldu behaved like brother and sister.

Woldu says: 'We made sure the children felt like she was their new mother before we started sleeping together. We didn't marry. We based our relationship on trust. We supported each other. She proved to be a fantastic mother to the girls; she was blessed. She didn't talk too much and she respected me.'

An expert at making *injera*, Letebirhan has a welcoming and seemingly permanent smile. She has a rolling and pronounced limp as a result of a botched childhood operation by traditional healers. When she was six years old, she developed a swelling on her upper thigh that eventually went septic. Traditional medicine was used. A blade was placed in a fire, then pushed into the infected area. She says, 'I have always had a limp but it has never stopped me doing what I wanted in my life.'

Letebirhan was now central to a family facing catastrophe. The land around Lahama had become a parched moonscape. Death was everywhere. As September rolled into October of 1984, Woldu remembered his friends and neighbours in the village were 'falling like leaves'. In a low mumble, he remembers: 'The land and the sky had collided. It was darkness. Two bodies were taken out from the *sekela* next to ours. The next day two more in another hut. The village was starving to death, the cattle were dying.'

The villagers of Lahama knew the only way to survive was to flee, to escape the curse that had fallen on their once fertile valley. 'The entire village decided we would leave as one,' Woldu says. 'Someone had heard that food aid was being handed out in Mekele so we decided to take everything we could carry and leave. No one stayed, no one at all. Everyone fled from the village, everyone. Rich, poor, men, women and children. Everyone. People were terrified that if they stayed in Lahama there would be no one left to bury them.'

The dignity of a Christian burial is a cornerstone of these mountain people's beliefs. Woldu packed the family's meagre possessions, their pots and pans and blankets, on a donkey. He then lowered himself down to the dry earth and hauled first Birhan and then little Silas onto his shoulders. With one perched on each side, their bony arms wrapped around his neck, he walked. Letebirhan, along with Lemlem and Azmera, drove their five goats, ox, cow and calf in front.

Woldu says: 'It would normally take me around five hours to walk to Kwiha – with the children it took nearly seven. We had to keep stopping for breaks. Letebirhan's leg was hurting. I had to encourage her every step of the way. Our bellies were empty.

'I turned to Letebirhan and said: "If I die you bury me, if you die I'll bury you." It sounds very strange but people were dying on the pathways or just walking off and disappearing to die. It took a long time but we thought we were heading at last for food. I thought the family would be saved.'

Letebirhan says she remembers their flight from Lahama like yesterday: 'We walked slowly. We had to take rest and breaks because of my bad leg. We were praying for God's help; we put our lives in the hands of the Almighty.'

The group of starving, God-fearing Lahama villagers and the remnants of their herds crested the ridge above Kwiha hoping for salvation. Instead they were greeted with a vision from hell. The blur of movement on the windswept plain below them gradually came into focus. Then they heard blast after blast of the Tigrayan horn that announces death in the family. In a wide swathe around war-ravaged Mekele were some 85,000 stick-thin people in rags. Proud Tigrayan farming folk like Woldu and his family lay dying. A low pall of woodsmoke lay over the plateau like a shroud. The putrid stench of urine and excrement was overpowering.

Woldu led his family towards the little market town and truck stop of Kwiha, little more than a church and a collection of brick shacks and huts looking down on Mekele's airstrip. It was a familiar place, where in the good times he had sold his firewood and delicious honey. The bedraggled and terrified young family found a patch of dust among the multitude near a feeding centre in the shadow of St Mary's Church, the spire of which dominates the town. They squatted down with their few blankets and pans, their animals tethered close by, and placed themselves at the mercy of the Lord.

His intense stare unblinking, Woldu shakes his head: 'It was a sight I never thought I would see. People dying everywhere. Even those who were rich and had lots of cows and oxen were dying. If a wife died the husband didn't cry because he didn't have the energy.'

The cold nights were punctuated with the piercing cackle and shriek of hyenas attracted by the stench of death. Sometimes they fed on the human flesh of those who died in the night. At other times they preyed on the living. In the brightness of day vultures rode the thermals waiting to prey on human carrion. The children at first watched the vultures with horror, but they soon grew used to the scavengers' shadows as they passed overhead.

In a dirty smock Lemlem, the eldest at around seven, helped Letebirhan look after baby Silas, who had only just started eating solid food. Though there was precious little of that around. A strong child used to long days with the herds in the mountains, Lemlem had already assumed the proud stoicism of Tigrayan mountain women. Azmera, around five, was cut from a similar mould. Azmera loved to baby little Birhan, still a toddler, who liked to chatter to everyone while her elder sisters were happier to remain quieter, in their own worlds.

'We huddled together under a blanket in the open air,' says Woldu, finding words difficult now. 'It was freezing cold at night. I would try and sleep sitting up so that I could wrap a blanket around my back and around Birhan and Azmera, lying each side of me. The wind was strong and would blow dust in my face all night. The hyenas screamed in the darkness. It was hell. When we woke up people were lying dead around us.'

Woldu and the other farming families tried hard to keep their herds of livestock. They knew that once their animals were gone they would struggle to feed themselves in the future. He sold the ox, the cow and her calf soon after arriving at Kwiha and bought wheat and some wood for a fire. His donkey and goats followed soon afterwards. They were eating a handful of grain each a day but it soon started to run out. Then they had no food at all; they were begging but there was nothing.

'People were dying all around us,' Woldu murmurs, 'at least 10 every day, even rich families from the village. Friends who had 20 cows and 10 oxen, who had given Alemetsehay honey and yoghurt when she had her babies, were dying. People were employed to collect the dead bodies every morning and take them to the church. They were buried in one big hole. There was no dignity. Such a small amount of food could have saved people from death, such a small amount. My children were crying with fear. Letebirhan was crying. I was crying.'

Birhan's family had already gone through the initial stages of hunger in Lahama. The first, nagging hunger pangs last only a few days. With no other nourishment the body then sets about eating itself, a stage known as catabolysis. It is the physiology of the starving. First the fat reserves are consumed, then the muscle tissue. The buttocks disappear, the limbs become desperately thin and the faces emaciated.

Atrophy (the wasting away) of the stomach weakens the perception of hunger. Victims of starvation are often too weak to sense thirst so become dehydrated. Any movement becomes painful due to the muscle wasting and also the dry, cracked skin that is caused by severe dehydration. With a weakened body, diseases become commonplace. Men become impotent, women's periods stop and breast milk can no longer be produced. Vitamin deficiencies lead to anaemia, beriberi, pellagra and scurvy, which in turn may cause diarrhoea, skin rashes and heart failure. The starving become irritable and lethargic. Then fatigue sets in. Minds become unfocussed and irrational. Soon even those things are replaced with a blank indifference. Hair falls out in clumps, pulse rate and blood pressure fall and the body loses its ability to shiver. Hypothermia and a raft of diseases, including tuberculosis and flu, claim some. Others can hold on for weeks before perishing.

In the midst of this, Woldu pulled his family closer to him in the bitter mountain wind. Despite the sheer horror of existence in Mekele his faith in the Lord remained unshakeable.

'I prayed to God over and over.

'I asked him: "What are you going to do with me?

'Please rescue me and my children. Lord... Please."'

THE CLOSEST
THING TO
HELL ON EARTH

THE TWIN OTTER light aircraft banked steeply above the teeming mass of starving humanity, before coming into land at Mekele's makeshift airstrip. Staring in disbelief from the windows were the BBC's Southern Africa Correspondent Michael Buerk, cameraman Mohamed 'Mo' Amin and the BBC Radio's East Africa Correspondent Mike Wooldridge.

It was October 19, 1984 and even experienced news reporters like Buerk and Wooldridge, who had witnessed much of Africa's recent troubled history, were shocked by the magnitude of the human tragedy that lay before them. They had flown into the 20th century's worst humanitarian disaster. The bundles of apparently discarded rags they had seen from the air were, in fact, people. Tens of thousands of skeletal and starving people, in reality fervently religious Tigrayan farming families known for their proud dignity, were, it seemed, just waiting to die.

Wooldridge recalls: 'Although we had all worked on famine stories before nothing had quite prepared us for what we found. The sheer scale of the famine was unbelievable, and the fact that people of all ages, not just the young and old, were starving was new to us.'

'The roads were just littered with dying people. It was extraordinary; it was just on such a huge scale,' Buerk later told British newspaper the *Observer*. 'People suddenly realized they were going to die and this huge mass migration started. It tipped very quickly. They tended to congregate along the spinal road that led north from Addis where they thought relief would get to them. There was this feeling that apart from the few agencies working there, no one knew about this thing. The speed of the deterioration of the people was so rapid that it had overtaken everyone.'

Squatting in a pitiful huddle under filthy blankets amid the teeming crowd, Woldu, Letebirhan and Birhan and her sisters would have heard the whirr of the Twin Otter's engines as the light aircraft came into land. Although it was possibly the first plane Birhan – and probably many others – had ever seen close up, few took any notice.

'We were too hungry to care what was happening around us,' Woldu explains. 'We didn't even know if it was night or day. I don't remember the plane. I was too busy searching for scraps of food and some clean water. We were starving.'

Woldu recalls the stench being horrendous, a mixture of woodsmoke, human waste and eucalyptus. Water was scarce. The main source was now a dribble from the fast-drying Elala riverbed to the north of Mekele and that was used by humans as well as animals both as a toilet and to wash in. In addition, most people had little or no food.

Everyone and seemingly everything was covered in a film of grey, clinging dust. Their once bright white *gabi* shawls and tunics were now dirty and torn – sometimes so tattered that they failed to protect the wearer's modesty. The wind howled across the exposed plateau ringed by rocky crags leached a grey brown by the elements. The nights high in the mountains could drop below freezing. There were pinpricks of flames dotting the landscape where families had made little cooking fires. Then as the early morning mists were burnt off by the sun, the heat became intense and unforgiving. Huge black flies swarmed everywhere. Those that were strong enough attempted to swat them away for a brief respite from the torment. Moments later the insects were back in a dark cloud to goad the starving. Many people were just too weak to bother with the irritant. Children wept with the pain of their bodies digesting themselves. Their parents – at least those with strength left – prayed or begged for help. People were dying in their droves.

For Birhan and her family, 'home' was now a scrap of dirt close to a low stone wall in Kwiha on a dusty plain next to the airstrip, around 10km (6 miles) outside of Mekele. The Derg had set up military checkpoints around the city, effectively shutting it off from the outside world.

Woldu would spend much of the day searching for scraps of food using the few birr he had gained from selling his livestock. Letebirhan would try to amuse the children.

Woldu was having to use all of his ingenuity to keep his family alive. He bought a sack of wheat with some of the birr and rationed it between the family at a handful each a day. They baked it on a little pan over a eucalyptus twig fire. But soon the money and then the wheat ran out and Woldu was in despair. His family was becoming increasingly weak, their skin covered in lesions, their joints bulbous and swollen, and their limbs like sticks.

Little Birhan had always loved drawing pictures with a twig in the sand. She was always doing it to keep amused. Suddenly she stopped. Woldu and Letebirhan cradled Birhan, Lemlem,

Azmera and Silas beneath filthy blankets. They barely moved. They were so pale and had no energy.

'I thought the end was coming for us,' Woldu says. 'That our suffering would end with death on that plain.'

Every morning people would come around to collect the bodies of those who had died overnight. They were taken to the church and given a Christian funeral. There were dozens of them: men, women and children, under blankets or bound in sackcloth for burial in the local custom.

'I don't remember much about that time.' Birhan comments almost 27 years later. 'Perhaps it is because I don't want to remember and it is locked away in the back of my mind. But I don't think I'm blocking it out. I just can't remember and I'm glad I don't. I have spoken to my father and Lemlem about what things were like in Kwiha then. The suffering of my family and millions of others was dreadful. I've seen the videos of the starving. People picking individual grains of wheat from the dust; it was terrible. I know I was one of those people. There were millions like me, millions.'

The Western media had already reported that a wide swathe of Ethiopia was experiencing a chronic famine. Buerk himself had filed a harrowing piece from Soddu in the southern Ethiopia province of Wollaita in the summer of 1984. He reported that thousands were dying every day. It was also the lead on the BBC's Nine O'Clock News and British independent TV station Central screened the hard-hitting documentary *Seeds of Despair* in July 1984. It recorded the first wave of famine victims at Korem, south of Mekele. The graphic images of the starving masses produced an outpouring of sympathy and the British public responded with £10 million in donations. Now the BBC team had persuaded the Derg's Ministry of Information to allow them to travel to drought-plagued Tigray. The epicentre of the famine, the mountains of the north were also a war zone where the Derg were fighting rebel movements. That meant that the starving were effectively cut off from the outside world.

Buerk was the BBC's man in Johannesburg, where he was covering the iniquities of the racially discriminatory apartheid system. And it was from there that he came to Ethiopia to follow up reports of severe famine. Buerk linked up in Nairobi with cameraman Amin. A respected photojournalist Amin helped smooth the bureaucracy on arriving in Addis Ababa.

'Mohammed Amin and I had for a few months been trying to gain access to the affected region,' Wooldridge remembers. 'But one of the problems was that the Ethiopian authorities were highly suspicious of journalists, as there had been instances of journalists who received transit visas to work on famine stories but instead had focussed on the war. Many myths exist about the attitude of the Ethiopian authorities; however some of them risked a lot, they cared a great deal and were a great help to us.'

Finally permission was granted and the men boarded the Twin Otter plane. After landing, the BBC team soon commandeered a lorry and turned left away from Kwiha to drive into Mekele along a bumpy stretch of road crowded with the starving and dying.

Along the way they were forced to stop several times to swerve around babies that had apparently been left abandoned in the road. The driver explained that the mothers were in fact watching from among the crowds, hoping the *farenjis* would take their children in and save their lives.

Buerk's coverage of southern Ethiopia that summer hadn't prepared him for the apocalyptic sight that greeted him at

Mekele. The horrors that he witnessed on the arid plains there were beyond imagination. Desperate peasants, who had walked to the city's feeder roads from Tigray's interior after hearing of the by now completely overwhelmed feeding stations, were literally dying on their feet.

He witnessed a group of women picking through a pile of donkey's dung looking for undigested grain to eat. Buerk describes how aid officials had taken over a compound of tin sheds surrounded by a low wall. Forty people died on the day the BBC filmed there alone. They captured the appalling suffering as best they could.

'It's difficult to express the inadequacy I felt,' Buerk later commented. 'You take refuge in the technicalities of filming, finding sequences, working out the logistics and so on.'

The shell-shocked TV crew overnighted in the imperial-era Castle Hotel on a hilltop overlooking the town where black kites soared above the cyprus trees and flowering shrubs in the grounds. Because of the scenes he had just witnessed, Buerk was surprised to find plenty of food being served at the hotel including *injera* bread and *tibbs*, a gristly fried lamb.

The next day the BBC team found an improvised shelter for babies being run by an Anglo–Swiss nurse named Claire Bertschinger, who worked for the International Committee of the Red Cross. Bertschinger had been inspired to take up nursing after watching the 1958 film *The Inn of the Sixth Happiness* starring the Hollywood actor Ingrid Bergman as an English missionary in China. Claire remembers thinking: 'That's what I want to do.'

After graduating in Medical Anthropology from England's Brunel University she trained as a nurse. She then followed her dream and volunteered to work in a series of war-torn regions, for the Red Cross. In July 1984, she was posted to Tigray to help run a supplementary feeding centre for children around 5km

(3 miles) from the centre of Mekele as the summer rains failed. It was a different clinic from the one that Woldu queued at in nearby Kwiha.

Emergency rations of flour, beans, butter oil and sugar were flown into Mekele every four to six weeks on a C–130 Hercules chartered by the Red Cross. Bertschinger never knew when it would arrive or how much help it would bring. It was never enough to feed the starving multitude, though. The only other way food could reach the civil war-ravaged area was by armed convoy but the aid trucks could be months apart. 'People didn't know what was happening here. We were hidden. That's what it felt like. The world didn't know.'

Bertschinger vividly remembers the starving jumping in front of land cruisers and trucks winding along the roads into Mekele. 'We were told by local people that these hungry, suffering people who had lost their loved ones weren't trying to kill themselves. They thought they must have committed some evil and that the devil was now on their backs. They were hoping the trucks would knock the devil off.'

Surrounded by thousands of starving people and with limited supplies, Bertschinger's soul-searching task was to choose which children to feed at her centre. She remembers a rare occasion when she had some leftover food and mashed it up to give to those who had been waiting patiently at the centre's gates. When some spilled on the ground there was a rush of people who bent down and licked it up from the dust. She was devastatingly aware that those children she turned away might not survive the night. Each morning the young nurse had to select 50 or 60 starving or sick children from astonishingly patient lines of 1,200 equally unwell youngsters and their parents. To choose who would live and who would die. The selection procedure took two long hours under the blazing sun. Bertschinger would put her hand around each child's arm to feel how malnourished he or she was. With a nod of her head they were either in or out. She chose the ones whom she believed had the best chance of survival. Often those most malnourished, who would be dead within one or two days, were turned away. They wouldn't respond to supplementary feeding. She couldn't understand why the starving Tigrayans were so orderly. People would tug gently at her, but remained largely calm.

'It was terrible to see people brought so low,' she wrote later in her memoirs *Moving Mountains*. 'They must have thought I was playing God... I felt guilty and ashamed that I could save so few and was sending most of them to certain death. I felt like a Nazi condemning innocent people to the death camps.'

Then Michael Buerk and the BBC cameras arrived. Mo Amin's camera tracked the nurse as she made her agonizing life or death judgements, down the lines of children, whose eyes stared blankly and hopelessly into the lens. Buerk then interviewed her.

'Making that decision day after day, does that do anything to you?' he asked. Outraged, Bertschinger snapped back: 'Yes, of course it does. What do you expect? It breaks my heart.' The BBC men moved on. Buerk remembers: 'I thought she was an angel; she thought I was a prat.'

Birhan says, 'It's funny to think that Michael [Buerk] and the TV cameras were so close to us then. Of course we had no idea they were there. We were all too weak and were sleeping outside a different feeding centre. Michael's cameras didn't film us. The family didn't even know what television was then.'

The BBC team flew onto nearby Korem where they witnessed more harrowing scenes of unimaginable human suffering. Cameraman Amin later remembered: 'There was this tremendous mass of people, groaning and weeping, scattered across the ground in the dawn mist.'

After Korem, Buerk spent the night in the comfort of Addis Ababa's Hilton Hotel with its plush bars, restaurants and a heated outdoor pool shaped like a cross. The hotel, then as now, is favourite with those paid to alleviate Ethiopia's hunger. Buerk admits feeling 'overwrought and full of disgust' at the sight of aid workers enjoying the hotel's varied menu and sampling the wine list. He also had his own sense of guilt to contend with. He later said of his Tigray assignment that as a journalist surrounded by the starving he couldn't think of a more useless occupation than his own.

As Buerk jetted out of Addis airport for the Kenyan capital of Nairobi, Birhan's family were still gathered by the crumbling stone wall among the dying and destitute. The stench of death was all around. Some 10km (6 miles) from Claire Bertschinger's feeding centre, the family preferred the comfort of being close to Kwiha's St Mary's Church.

As the chill of the night passed, Woldu would join the winding queues for food at a corrugated iron feeding centre in the little market town. As the sun rose Letebirhan would stay with the children while Woldu summoned the strength to search for food and water. He found none. The feeding centres were overrun and more hungry people came from the arid countryside every day.

Birhan and her sisters were now terribly weak. Their stomachs, empty of food, became distended and bloated. Their hair turned red and their skin became flaky and covered in lesions. They had rasping coughs and were plagued by diarrhoea. Other children on the hellish plateau had xerophthalmia, caused by Vitamin A deficiency, in which the whites of a child's eyes to turn muddy brown while the brown iris turns milky blue. The cornea then softens, the lens falls out and the whole eye begins to rot.

'People were dying around us every day,' Letebirhan says quietly. 'No child should have to see what our little ones witnessed at Kwiha… Of course, there were tears at times but they mostly were good girls. We were so proud of them… Soon they were too weak to cry anyway.'

The family now had no food left. And little strength. The only thing left was to pray for deliverance. Woldu says: 'People were crying: "God why are you punishing us? What have we done?" Everyone was praying to God to give them food. I promised to God that if my daughters and I safely made it back to the promised land – back to Lahama with the rains and crops in the fields – that if I arrived in the morning, he could kill me in the afternoon.'

Flying back to London from Nairobi with an eight-and-a half-minute cut of his first report, Buerk began writing his commentary over Amin's long-tracking shot of the misery of Korem. 'Dawn, and as the sun breaks through the piercing chill of night on the plain outside Korem it lights up a biblical famine, now, in the 20th century. This place, say workers here, is the closest thing to hell on earth. Thousands of wasted people are coming here for help. Many find death. They flood in every day from villages hundreds of miles away, dulled by hunger, driven beyond the point of desperation… 15,000 children here now suffering, confused, lost… Death is all around. A child or an adult dies every 20 minutes. Korem, an insignificant town, has become a place of grief.'

Buerk's calm and simple prose was sparse yet dignified. He punctuated the stark and shocking pictures with barely concealed anger and disgust for what humankind was allowing to happen to the children of Korem and Mekele, childen like Birhan and her sisters. The reports were all the more powerful for it. This was journalism that would quite simply help change the world.

A WORLD
AWARE

IN THE
LONG GRASS

PUNK ROCKER Bob Geldof slammed down the telephone receiver before bellowing a stream of coarse expletives at the top of his voice. Unshaven, with his straggly unkempt brown hair pushed back behind his ears, he had spent the afternoon of October 24, 1984, at his London record company, Phonogram, trying to push his latest single 'Dave'. Pete Townsend, guitarist with legendary British rock band The Who, thought it was one of the best songs of 1984, but the radio stations obviously disagreed. It was getting no airplay, so no one was buying it. Like the two previous singles of Geldof's band The Boomtown Rats, it had stiffed badly. The Irish band's seemingly effortless string of hits, including 1979 chart topper 'I Don't Like Mondays' had, it seemed, come to an end. The fickle pop world had moved on and the band was broke.

Still, he had come a long way from Dun Laoghaire, Ireland, where he had been born on October 5, 1951. After attending an exclusive Dublin Catholic private school, he had left Ireland for a time taking various hand-to-mouth jobs, before ending up in

Vancouver, where he worked as a music journalist for the *Georgia Straight* magazine. It was here that he had learned the true power of having a voice. His often opinionated columns led him to be sought out by the local media who wanted him to comment on various issues. 'Canada taught me that your level of effectiveness increased in direct proportion to your level of power,' Geldof says. 'The more people you knew, the more you could do.'

Back in Dublin in 1975 Geldof and some friends formed the punk/new wave group The Boomtown Rats, named after a gang of kids in an Oklahoma oil town described by folk singer Woody Guthrie in his autobiography.

The band had its first hit 'Lookin' After Number One' in 1977; 'Rat Trap' topped the singles chart in Britain in the next year. The loud-mouthed singer was now recognized wherever he went. The Rats looked as if they would become one of the most enduring of the new wave bands, and Geldof's celebrity soared once more as the band's single 'I Don't Like Mondays' was a global smash in 1979.

'Mondays' was written in response to a California school shooting during which 16-year-old Brenda Ann Spencer killed two adults and injured eight children and one police officer. Spencer showed no remorse and said she had opened fire on the innocents because, 'I don't like Mondays. This livens up the day.' Geldof's stark third verse lyrics contained the line *'And the lesson today is how to die'*. In the United States, fear of lawsuits and charges of bad taste kept the song off the radio. It was about the only major market in which it wasn't a massive hit.

By 1984, The Rats had finished another album, *In the Long Grass,* which they believed had three hit tracks on it. The title is an Irish expression: 'When you have not seen someone for a long time and you ask them where they have been they might reply, "Oh, I've been lying in the long grass"', Geldof says.

Pop music is transient, however, and fashions ebb and flow. It now it seemed that The Rats as a band was very much in the long grass. All three singles flopped and the group was now seen as over the hill. Geldof felt he had lost his way.

The dejected singer returned to his home in London's fashionable Chelsea in a state of blank resignation. Slumped on the sofa next to his beautiful blonde girlfriend, broadcaster Paula Yates, he switched on the TV to watch the *Six O'Clock News*. It was the fourth report on the bulletin that captured their attention, shocking them both into silence. They were witnessing hell on Earth.

There was the emaciated mother too weak to do anything but limply hold her child. A skeletal man holding a bundle of sacking that looked like a tightly wrapped package of old sticks but was in fact the shrunken body of his child. The gaunt faces of the children, their eyes huge with the consciousness of what was happening to them.

The haunting pictures from that broadcast – and another by Michael Buerk on October 25 – have stayed fresh in Geldof's mind for over quarter of a century. Both showed the horrors of Korem and Mekele, where thousands of kilometres away people like Birhan and her family lay starving in the dirt. It left the musician seething with rage and numbed with shame.

Yates burst into tears and ran upstairs to check on their 19-month-old baby, Fifi Trixibelle, who was sleeping peacefully in her cot. Geldof went up to bed but couldn't sleep. The ghastly vision that kept crowding his mind was of the blonde Red Cross nurse Claire Bertschinger having to play God. To choose which children would live and which would die. The stark images just wouldn't go away.

That night thousands of kilometres away, the freezing October wind whistled across the dry tableland outside Kwiha in the Ethiopian Highlands. Woldu huddled next to his daughters under the stars. Their bellies were empty like thousands of other Tigrayans and their desperate plight seemed hopeless. But now the world knew – millions were aware of their suffering.

At the time of the broadcast Geldof had little in-depth knowledge of Africa and development issues. He had never even heard of Eritrea, Ethiopia's secessionist northern province, but Michael Buerk's reports came at the precise moment when the singer's ferocious drive and vision needed a new direction. He was appalled at what he had seen. He had to do something. 'Doing nothing would mean you were complicit in murder. I know that's an extreme term but… people were dying.'

Geldof's first thought was to donate cash, which for many people would have been enough. After some consideration he realized that the situation required 'something more than the charitable impulse… it required an effort of self and all I could do, badly as it was turning out, was write a couple of tunes.'

He decided to do what he did best. To use his power as a musician and celebrity to make a difference – to raise public awareness of the horror happening in Ethiopia and hopefully raise much-needed funds while doing so.

Geldof picked up the phone and rang the very many friends and colleagues he had in the music industry. First came old friend Midge Ure from the band Ultravox. Then Sting, the charismatic singer from The Police, and Duran Duran's front man Simon Le Bon, who both jumped at the chance of taking part. Over the next few days a stream of other leading musicians came on board. Geldof's diary page from the time lists them: 'Eurythmics, Bananarama, Culture Club, Thompson Twins, Frankie Goes to Hollywood, Wham!, Sade, Paul Young and the Style Council.'

Gary Kemp, guitarist with synth pop band Spandau Ballet, remembers being accosted by Geldof in an antiques shop on Chelsea's fashionable King's Road the day after Buerk's report was broadcast. 'Geldof saw me and came in. He sucked the air out of the place and took over, as he does. He said, "Did you see the news last night?" He was clearly very moved. "Maybe if we got a few people together, yourselves, Duran and some others, would you be interested in making a record?" I said "Yeah, sure" – and that was it.'

Phonogram, Geldof's record company, agreed to waive its profits. Workers in the Phonogram factory would end up working on the single for free.

Geldof began fiddling around with parts of a song he had already worked on called 'It's My World'. He wanted his charity single to be a Christmas record and it would need some appropriate lyrics. The weekend after Buerk's landmark bulletins found Geldof in the back of a taxi on the way to visit a sick friend in Ireland where he scribbled out the lyrics to 'Do They Know It's Christmas?' He wrote fluently, with little crossing out. The words seemed to pour out of him.

'I wanted to make people think'. So, he wrote:

It's Christmas time,
there's no need to be afraid.
At Christmas time
we let in light and banish shade
And in our world of plenty
we can spread a smile of Joy
Throw your arms around the world
at Christmas time.
But say a prayer,
Pray for the other ones.
At Christmas time it's hard

but when you're having fun...
There's a world outside your window
and it's a world of dread and fear
Where the only water flowing is
the bitter sting of tears
Where the Christmas bells that are ringing
are the clanging chimes of Doom
Well, tonight thank God it's them instead of you.

And there won't be snow in Africa this Christmas time
The greatest gift they'll get this year is life.
Ohh...
Where nothing ever grows
No rain or rivers flow
Do they know it's Christmas time at all?

Here's to you...
Raise a glass for everyone
Here's to them
Underneath that burning sun
Do they know it's Christmas time at all?
Feed the world...
Feed the world...
Feed the world,
Let them know it's Christmas time again.
Feed the world,
Let them know it's Christmas time again.

Midge Ure added music to Geldof's heartfelt lyrics and Sunday November 25, 1984, was chosen as the day to record the song in a studio. More than a quarter of a century later Geldof would say he still heard the song every Christmas at supermarket Morrisons' meat counter alongside perennial festive favourites

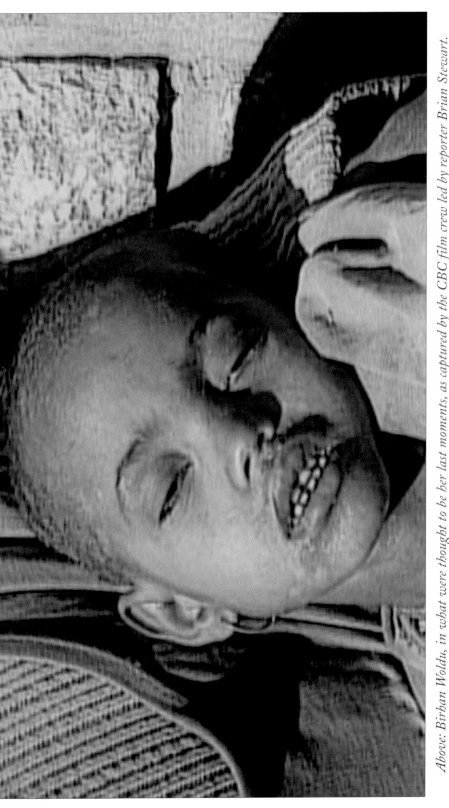

Above: Birhan Woldu, in what were thought to be her last moments, as captured by the CBC film crew led by reporter Brian Stewart. This image was broadcast at the Live Aid concerts in 1985. (CBC TV Archive Sales)

Right: Bloodthirsty dictator Mengistu Haile Mariam was leader of the Derg, the Communist military junta that governed Ethiopia from 1974 to 1987. Known by some as the 'Black Stalin', he murdered thousands during the Red Terror purges and his disastrous policies exacerbated the 1984 famine. (Rex Features/Sipa Press)

Above: Emperor Haile Selassie – Ethiopia's Negus Negast or 'King of Kings' – was said to come from an unbroken dynastic line stretching back to the biblical King Solomon and the Queen of Sheba. Also known as the 'Elect of God' and the 'Conquering Lion of Judah', he ruled feudal Ethiopia from 1916 to 1974 before he was deposed and murdered by the Derg. (Getty Images/Hulton Archive)

*Above: The famine fields of Mekele. An estimated one million Ethiopians died in the great famine. (Rex Features/Steve Bent/*Mail on Sunday*)*

Above: Birhan's father, Woldu Menamano, at the dilapidated mud hut where she was born in the remote village of Lahama in Tigray Province. (Oliver Harvey)

Above: Woldu poses with village children in Lahama, showing how he carried Birhan and Silas on their epic journey from the Lowlands after they were forcibly resettled in 1985. It was 1,300km (800 miles) back to their home in Tigray. (Oliver Harvey)

*Above: Birhan volunteering as a nurse at Mekele Health Centre in 2009. With her is Dame Claire Bertschinger (top centre), the nurse who featured in Michael Buerk's landmark BBC famine reports in 1984. (Arthur Edwards/*The Sun*)*

Above: Birhan and father Woldu at Kwiha on the patch of dust near a feeding centre, where the family slept in the open during the 1984 famine. Birhan's older sister Azmera died here during the great hunger. (Oliver Harvey)

Above: Brian Stewart with Birhan and her father, Woldu, taken when Birhan was aged about 13. (Birhan Woldu Collection)

Above: Live Aid – the 'Global Jukebox' – on July 13, 1985, at London's Wembley Stadium. It is estimated that 85 percent of the world's TV sets were tuned into it. (Getty Images)

Above: Bob Geldof at Live 8 on July 2, 2005. Moments later, billions around the world watched Birhan walk onto the stage in front of a giant image of herself close to death during the 1984 famine. (Rex Features/Richard Young)

Overleaf: Birhan near Gleneagles Hotel in Scotland, where G8 leaders were meeting to forge a deal for Africa just days after Live 8 in July, 2005. (Paul Edwards/The Sun)

from the 1970s' pop bands Slade and Wizard.

'I suppose it's not a bad tune,' he would grudgingly admit.

Michael Buerk's landmark reports hadn't just spurred a scruffy, down-on-his-luck pop star in Britain into action, though. His words – and the images accompanying them – were subsequently broadcast by 425 television stations around the world. The response was immediate – Buerk's report unleashing a tidal wave of private giving. International charity Save the Children Fund reported that its phones were jammed with people desperate to donate cash for Ethiopia's starving as soon as Buerk's reports were aired in Britain.

Over a billion people saw Buerk and Amin's landmark footage. It elicited the same massive response of tears, sympathy and giving wherever it was shown across the globe. In Australia Prime Minister Bob Hawke wept and in the US President Ronald Reagan was visibly moved and immediately pledged US $45 million. No single piece of journalism has arguably had such far-reaching effects. Michael Buerk's report was responsible for a global epidemic of charity and compassion.

Back in the famine fields of Mekele, Woldu and his young family were, of course, unaware of the emotion-charged whirlwind of humanitarianism sweeping across the planet. They had more immediate concerns.

Three-year-old Birhan had fallen desperately ill almost on the day of the BBC's broadcasts in Britain and the West. One morning in late October 1984, Woldu awoke to find her staring blankly into the mid-distance, her brow furrowed in the rising sun. Her pale skin was pulled taut against her skull, her limbs like matchwood. She had a rasping, death-rattle cough. He gently called out his daughter's name and watched with increasing anguish as she tried to get to her feet. She couldn't control her body. She was too weak. When she tried to stand, she staggered and fell; her muscles had wasted away and her legs were simply not strong enough to support her. Despite this, she tried again and again for what seemed like an age, then she finally stopped trying at all.

Letebirhan says, 'We could usually never stop Birhan talking. She was such a little chatterbox, it was a delight. When she fell silent on that plain, not uttering a word, we knew something was very wrong.'

Woldu scooped up into his arms the bundle of bones that was his adored daughter and took her to a tumbledown, corrugated tin-walled government clinic near their patch of dirt by St Mary's Church in Kwiha. She was given some sort of syrup by the local Ethiopian aid workers, but she could barely take it down she was so weak. They returned to Letebirhan and Lemlem, Azmera and Silas, but the syrup hadn't done Birhan any good. She was getting weaker and weaker. Woldu knew she needed proper medical help from a *farenji* doctor. He looked across at Letebirhan, who was now quietly weeping as Birhan's mouth lolled open, gasping, and her eyes rolled back in their sockets. The droning buzz of flies was all around. Her sisters, Lemlem and Azmera, began to sob and sniffle. It set off baby Silas who also started to wail.

Woldu knew that if he didn't get his daughter to a doctor she would soon be dead. The outpouring of compassion in the West might possibly have come too late for Birhan.

15 MINUTES
TO LIVE

THE BESIEGED Catholic nuns at the little grey stone clinic St Vincent de Paul were overwhelmed every day by the clamour for help from the deathly ill and hungry. Gathered by the hundred along the clinic's outer wall, they sought some shade from the glare of the Ethiopian sun while patiently waiting their turn to be seen. Inside were trained Western medics and life-saving modern medicine. For many it was worth the wait. News of this rare beacon of hope had reached some of the thousands on the famine fields around Kwiha.

Woldu knew the *farenji* clinic in the dustbowl hamlet of Latchi on the far side of Mekele was his daughter Birhan's last hope. He had decided with Letebirhan that she would remain among the filth and degradation of Kwiha with Lemlem, Azmera and Silas, while he sought help for their dying child.

At first light, as the shimmering dawn begin to burn off the morning mist shrouding the valleys of Tigray, Woldu gathered up the pitiful bundle of skin and bone that was his cherished little girl. Birhan was barely conscious now, not even able to mumble her prayers. Woldu carefully wrapped Birhan in a dirty shawl and strapped her to his back. With all the strength his hunger-ravaged body could muster, Woldu set off across the desolate plateau in a half-running lollop, his daughter limply wrapping her arms around his neck. The clutch of corrugated iron-roofed stone huts that make up Latchi is around 15km (9 miles) away from Kwiha across the rugged Highlands.

Everywhere father and daughter passed the dead and the dying, the young and the old, rich and poor. In places Woldu noticed that patches of dirt were darker against the fine yellow soil. These still moist areas were where fresh graves – often mass graves of the famine's latest victims – had been dug that morning. He knew that he had to hurry now and took a shortcut from the escarpment down a treacherous path used usually by the sure-footed goats. With fist-sized rocks rolling beneath his tyre-rubber sandals he strode on into the scorched expanse of the valley below.

The Catholic clinic, sheltered by towering eucalyptus trees, looked down from the far slopes with the seemingly endless African blue sky behind. It was still morning when Woldu and Birhan arrived, but already a seething mass of people had gathered. Some had that resigned stare of those who know death is inevitable; others still had the strength to plead with the guards at the wrought iron gates for admittance.

Security guard Tesfay Beri, now in his 50s, still mans the clinic's rusting gates as he did during the dark days of the 1984 famine. He remembers well the queues of desperate people in the dust and heat. People would come from far and wide clutching their children in a bid to save their lives. The clinic was greatly oversubscribed and Tesfay had to turn people away. Squinting in the midday sun, his bird-like features heavily lined and taut against his bony face, he recalled: 'We had to tell them there was no room, which was a very

84

upsetting thing to have to do. They were very tired and desperate but we had to keep them back and maintain order. Many people simply died outside the gate. They were terrible times.'

Woldu and Birhan were among those wretched souls who arrived too late to be seen that day. Woldu was told that the clinic was full. 'They turned me away and told us we would have to wait until the next day. Birhan was so weak and couldn't utter a word. My heart sank. We slept out in the open under my shawl. I held her close.'

Woldu managed to get a handful of wheat from a kind stranger, but Birhan wasn't able to eat. He knew he was losing her. It was essential she saw a doctor – it was now simply a matter of her life or death.

The mountains were slowly cloaked in darkness. Woldu slept fitfully on the hard ground. He woke with a start at 3am, rose quickly, and in very little time he had shuffled to the front of the dimly lit clinic to rejoin the queue of the diseased and malnourished. It was still pitch black and unbearably cold, so much so that all he could do was shiver as he held his child. This time there were just 10 families in front of him giving him hope that Birhan might receive the help that she so desperately needed. She didn't stir in his arms but he could feel her warm breath against his cheek in the mountain chill: she was still clinging desperately to life. The first rays of the luminous orange morning sun shone over the far peaks as the guards stirred at the clinic gates.

'We waited and waited as it got lighter and warmer,' Woldu painfully relates, his voice breaking with emotion. 'The queue was getting longer but we managed to keep our place. Birhan just got weaker. No one came to help us; I didn't know what to do. I tried to get her to stand, to keep her alive, but she flopped down by the wall. Then she lay completely still. There was no heartbeat. I felt she had died in my arms, her eyes rolled back in her head, her eyelids remained half open. She seemed to have stopped breathing completely.'

Woldu was too distraught to notice the *farenji* camera crew moving down the line of waiting people. However the despairing father and his dying child captured the attention of the dark-haired figure dressed in a sand-coloured safari-style jacket, a reporter's notebook clutched in his hand. The man was seasoned CBC foreign correspondent Brian Stewart. With him were French cameraman Philippe Billard, sound recordist John Axelson and the team's leader Producer Tony Burman, who was taking still pictures. The BBC reports had seen news teams scrambled to Ethiopia from across the globe. A roving correspondent based in CBC's London bureau, Stewart had a 'patch' which included turbulent Africa and the Middle East. He believed his experience in conflict zones had prepared him for the shock of Ethiopia's Great Famine. Today he admits that couldn't have been further from the truth.

By October 28, 1984, Stewart and his team were in the famine epicentre of Mekele. They had heard of the desperate scenes at Latchi's St Vincent de Paul clinic and how the Sisters there were overwhelmed by the sheer numbers descending on them. At about 9.30 on a windy and bitingly cold morning, Billard got to work capturing the devastation and human suffering. Those arriving had often walked two or three days to get to the clinic and were exhausted, a great many had died along the way. The clinic was overrun with parents, people like Woldu, who were bringing in sick and starving children.

Stewart recalls, 'We began moving along the wall, talking to mothers. By chance, in one wide shot I only noticed long afterwards can be seen the first picture of three-year-old Birhan, cradled in her father's arms. As Birhan and her father reached a wall I noticed her slumping to the pavement and called a nurse but it seemed too late.'

The images the CBC men captured show Birhan's delicate mouth lolling wide, her eyes open but seemingly blind. Her sallow, yellowed skin is stretched like crepe paper over her tiny skull, her limbs are mere bone and sinew.

Father and daughter were rushed to a row of simple stone huts beside the clinic where only the most sick were treated and sheltered. One of the centre's nuns was captured by Billard on camera placing her hand on Birhan's face and neck.

In an Irish brogue the Sister proclaims: 'The child will die very soon. The child has pneumonia. The child is very malnourished. This child is dying and nothing will save this child now. She will die here. Maybe within 15 minutes. There isn't anything we can do at this point for the child.'

Stewart and the CBC team pulled away. The journalist remembers: 'I was shaken because I really believed we were seeing her die before us. We left, to at least allow her dignity in death. Her grave was already being dug outside, alongside thousands of other victims.'

Down the years Woldu has replayed that dreadful moment through his mind again and again. In a barely audible whisper he recalls: 'I knelt down and hugged Birhan. She was gone; she stopped moving. Her eyes were open, but she wasn't able to see. I couldn't feel her breath.

'I put her down by a wall as it was meaningless to keep my place in the queue for treatment. I didn't want to be standing there with a dead body. There were so many people behind me with children who were very ill.

'I didn't notice people were filming me, I felt so terrible and sad. Then the nurse rushed her into the clinic. They said there was nothing they could do. I couldn't feel a heartbeat. Birhan was dead in my arms.'

Birhan's ragged funeral shroud was laid out. The nuns had left Woldu alone to spend his final moments with his little daughter. Wracked with grief, Woldu now held Birhan for the final time. He wept and felt the shame of not being able to give her the dignity of a Christian funeral himself. 'I didn't even have a shovel to bury her. Where would I find one? That was my sadness, I couldn't bury my little Birhan. It was no way for a father to let down his daughter. I couldn't think with grief let alone pray.' Then, he felt something as he gripped her emaciated arm that was little more than bone. Was his mind playing tricks on him? He held her by the wrist once more and there it was again. A tiny pulse, a soft heartbeat. Birhan was still alive. Frantically, he called a nurse over, grabbing the *farenji*'s hand to place it on Birhan's neck. The nurse was shocked to feel a pulse. She gave the child a rehydration injection.

Woldu shakes his head and adds: 'Birhan might already have been buried at that point. She would have been buried alive. It made me wonder how many other children had been buried but were not really dead.'

Hours later the CBC crew called back into the clinic on the way back from filming more scenes of devastation around Mekele. They were expecting to attend the funeral of the wasted little girl they had seen dying. Brian Stewart recalls: 'I was astonished to find what seemed a near miracle. We found Birhan alive in the arms of one of the sisters. I couldn't believe my eyes.' The nurse said she thought the child would now live and was responding after a series of rehydration shots. Stewart remembers the facilities in the row of stone huts where Birhan was now convalescing were primitive but that the nuns were attentive, dedicated and highly experienced in emergency care. Birhan was in good hands.

'I was overwhelmed with emotion,' Stewart readily confesses today. 'I'd expected the worst and for the first time in days I saw this burst of hope. Before then I hadn't seen one good story in Ethiopia, nothing that gave any hope whatsoever.

That's when Birhan's story first occurred to me as possibly symbolic of Ethiopia's ability to survive this nightmare as long as it received help from the outside world. I thought if she can make it, maybe the world will respond.'

Birhan can recall little from those hellish days: 'I don't dream about those dark times when I nearly died. I was lucky I was not a grown-up, I was lucky I didn't see all those ghastly things. But I would never forget those nurses who saved my life. They were like magical figures to me.'

Woldu lay next to Birhan on the soft mattress in the little stone hut. He saw the bodies of two dead children removed from a neighbouring hut. He didn't need reminding of the frailty of life on the plains of Mekele. She was barely conscious for three days. There was no movement, no words from the previously chattering toddler. Then her eyes opened a little. Woldu was stunned. A week later she could walk. 'It was unbelievable. Birhan's survival was a miracle,' Woldu murmurs. 'It was God's power, God loves her. He postponed her death. I saw so many people die but she survived. God allowed her to live for a reason.'

The CBC team flew back to Addis to edit Billard's astonishing images of Birhan against Stewart's evocative words for a series of reports. Both Billard and Stewart fought constant fatigue and emotional stress; they had witnessed so many deaths. Amid the clutter of a room in Addis's Hilton, CBC editor Colin Dean had to splice the reports together. Stewart described it as the most emotionally upsetting job of all.

Dean had lugged seven cases of editing equipment weighing upwards of 300kg (660lb) from London to the suite in the Addis Hilton. 'It seemed so incongruous to be staying in such luxury with such wonderful food when so many people were starving to death nearby,' Dean recalls. When Stewart and the CBC team brought their pictures in from the north Dean was truly horrified by what he saw. He had to force himself to banish his feelings temporarily to do his job. Soon he was editing the shocking frames of Birhan slipping towards death.

'I had to make notes of what I was seeing to make an edit. It seems terribly, terribly callous now but next to a particularly stark image of a dying child I would jot down three stars and write, "Great shot". I remember those shots of Birhan, they were terribly upsetting. It didn't reduce me to tears then, I had to get the job done. Even now it's quite difficult to look back and talk about it. Some of the stuff was too horrendous to send back to the office. Toronto wouldn't have run it. I had to put the awful images out of my mind, I was there to do a job, but it gets to you in the end.'

Tony Burman was forced to tape Stewart's first edited piece to his back and smuggle it out from Addis to Nairobi for the satellite feed in case regime officals attempted to seize them. In the first report from Mekele broadcast by CBC on November 1, horrified viewers saw starved corpses in the streets, an emaciated child with his head in his hands in despair. The nightmare scenes were impossible to erase from the mind and Stewart's words moving in the extreme.

'As each week passes, the hordes of famine victims in northern Ethiopia multiply in this endless, silent, frightening march for food, a spectacle hard to believe for our age. To some it's more an image of the great plagues of famines of the medieval world. To others, more science fiction, a projection of a crumbling world after a nuclear holocaust.'

It was the pictures in a later report of little Birhan surviving against all odds which had the greatest impact on a disbelieving public when they were screened by CBC in Canada and in the United States by NBC. Stewart says that all those watching the reports saw something they would never forget. Something they had never imagined. Like Buerk's BBC reports, the CBC films provoked an outpouring of raw emotion in Canada. They bewildered and shocked Canada's new UN ambassador, Stephen Lewis, who was just weeks into the job. His family collectively wept as they watched the CBC footage. New Democratic Party member Lewis said later: 'I had a lifetime of experience around Africa and I had been through the Biafran civil war and I'd seen famine and starvation in Eastern Nigeria. I'd never seen anything like these images. I was completely dumbstruck by it.'

At the UN's New York headquarters he found that months of warning over the famine by aid groups and the Ethiopian government had been ignored. 'No one was talking about it ... in diplomatic and bureaucratic circles,' Lewis comments but Birhan's tortured image helped change that. In his first speech before the General Assembly, Lewis attempted to alert the delegates to the enormity of Ethiopia's tragedy. He railed: 'What must come now is a Herculean effort on the part of all member nations to address those conditions which give rise to the crisis.'

Canada's new Conservative Prime Minister Brian Mulroney was as outraged by CBC's harrowing reports of Birhan and the other suffering children as Lewis. 'It was a calamity that was unfolding before our very eyes and nothing was happening. I thought someone else was going to do something, the US or the UK. We didn't know exactly what we were going to do except that we were going to step in and provide some leadership.'

Cold War politics meant Western governments were reluctant to aid Ethiopia's Marxist leader Colonel Mengistu Haile Mariam. In the first week of November 1984, Canada broke rank. Foreign Minister Joe Clark, rerouted a return flight from India to Addis. He was the first Western official to arrive following the shock waves caused by the media's famine reports, ahead of even UN leaders. Clark met up with Stewart and his team and viewed their shocking footage in the Hilton editing suite. Clark promised demoralized aid groups that help was on its way. Mengistu asked

Canada to become Ethiopia's bridge to the West. The Canadian government gave more than CAN $50 million at once. The public trauma unleashed a wave of humanitarian giving, many citing the shocking pictures of Birhan as a reason for action. There was a pandemic of fund-raising, ranging from politicians to pop stars, farmers to college kids, raising millions of dollars with the poorest – the Inuit in Canada's far north – giving most per capita.

Thanks to reporters Michael Buerk and Brian Stewart Ethiopia's catastrophe had gone from being one of the world's most forgotten crises to its best known. News crews were dispatched from across the globe to get their own eyewitness reports from Tigray's starvation zone. Ignorance was no longer an excuse.

As the West finally emerged from its apparent indifference to her homeland, Birhan was still recovering in the tiny stone hut outside the Latchi clinic. In the first week of November Woldu received news from Letebirhan still squatting on the bare earth with Lemlem, Azmera and baby Silas under the spire of St Mary's. A friend from Lahama had walked to the Latchi clinic to inform Woldu that five-year-old Azmera was gravely malnourished. Woldu left Birhan in the care of a fellow patient and made the 30km (19 mile) round trip to fetch Azmera in a day. He was delighted to see Letebirhan and his other daughters again but knew from experience he would have to move quickly.

One of Birhan's earliest memories is of lying in the unfamiliar fly-blown shack at Latchi with her sister. Birhan remembers Azmera's chocolate-coloured skin and the long plait she had at the back of her scalp fashioned like many children in the mountains.

Azmera was given high-calorie milk drinks and flatbread but remained very weak. She would entertain Birhan by playing with her lips as she lay convalescing in bed. 'I was sick but she would make me laugh by flipping my lips and making me go "blubber, blubber, blubber",' Birhan says, her eyes moist. 'She cared for me as a big sister, I really looked up to her.'

It was now the third week of November and Birhan and Azmera had grown stronger. It was time to rejoin the rest of the family back in Kwiha.

As the mountain winds roared, Stewart and the CBC cameras were present to witness Birhan and Azmera being led by the hand by Woldu as they passed through the gates of the Latchi clinic. Stewart remembers: 'The pictures of Birhan and her father and sister leaving the clinic and heading into the storm really haunted me afterwards. I was worried about their ultimate fate but was unable to stay around as we had to get off to other locations.'

Some *farenjis* from the clinic drove the family back to Kwiha. Birhan and Azmera were terrified at the prospect of their first ride in a motor car. 'It was like magic, we had only been on a donkey before,' Birhan recalls. 'Azmera was crying hysterically because as we moved down the road she thought the trees were coming towards us, moving, and were going to crash into us.' When they arrived back, Woldu led his daughters to the low wall beneath St Mary's, where Letebirhan, Lemlem and Silas waited. Woldu went back to begging and queuing for scraps of food and searching for shelter.

The CBC team were in Ethiopia for a further six weeks that winter. The outpouring of disgust and sympathy across Canada meant the network was desperate for more coverage. It subsequently dedicated a whole week to covering the African famine. Back in Addis Colin Dean was editing every second of the raw footage shot by the team in the field. The clattering sound of the editing equipment kept Stewart awake in the next room. Dean was working against tight deadlines at breakneck speed. He had no time for mistakes and had to view hour after hour of heartbreaking images for days on end. Stewart recalls: 'What we saw once, twice, Colin witnessed 50 times. I found he was close to tears on many occasions.'

Emotionally overwhelmed by the experience, and unable to sleep, Dean stayed up one night and put together his own music video as a memorial to victims of the famine. Father-of-two Dean explains: 'It just happened in the middle of the night and wasn't ever intended to be screened.'

He was listening to a compilation of songs on his Walkman as he worked when the haunting ballad 'Drive' by American new wave group The Cars rung out. Its poignant opening keyboard refrain gave way to bassist Benjamin Orr softly singing, *'Who's gonna tell you when it's too late, who's gonna tell you things aren't so great...'* Dean says the lyrics immediately resonated with him. 'It's a love song about being driven home at the end of the evening. The children in the film weren't even going to make it through the night.'

He set the evocative music to the images of the dying children, their pleading eyes the ones that he had stared into for hour upon hour while editing. One of the children towards the end of the tape seemingly breathing her last was a slumped, skeletal little girl whose wasted features and forlorn milky eyes radiated hopelessness.

It was clearly the gaunt and pained features of Birhan Woldu. The girl who had come back from the dead.

DO THEY KNOW IT'S CHRISTMAS?

RED CROSS NURSE Claire Bertschinger squinted hard as she stared at the tiny black dot in the deep blue vastness of the Ethiopian horizon. Gradually the speck became larger and larger in the sky above Mekele and she could hear the low drone of its propeller-driven engines. As the aircraft bore down on the dusty landing strip, Bertschinger could make out the green khaki and grey livery and then as it swooped low over the parched hills, the famous red, white and blue roundel of the Royal Air Force (RAF) painted on its fuselage.

It was the first week of November 1984, just 10 days after Michael Buerk's landmark reports, and salvation had come. The world had finally woken up to the horrors of Tigray. Today Claire admits that all she could think was, 'We're saved. We're saved'.

Driving out to the landing strip to meet the RAF plane, the young nurse was hauled aboard by the crew for a mug of hot tea and Marmite sandwiches on delicious white bread. A little bit of suburban England had arrived amid the misery of Tigray. The officers apologized for only having day-old white bread, but to Bertschinger this bread was manna from heaven. Cut off from the outside world, the young woman was unaware that she had featured in Buerk's TV reports and that international charities had since been flooded by donations from the public. But within a week more and more planes could be heard overheard and within a fortnight she was able to double the numbers at her feeding centre.

A makeshift town of army-surplus-style tents sprung up on the bleak plain of the dying around Mekele. The international media was also arriving in droves. The picture most wanted was the 'Angel of Mekele' with a starving child, the white nurse cradling a black baby.

Having now witnessed the bountiful effects of being filmed by the BBC she didn't mind acquiescing. She had also received letters from around the globe simply addressed to 'Sister Claire, Red Cross, Mekele, Ethiopia'. The new-found supplies and shelter at Mekele were proving encouragement for more of the starving and needy to leave their rural villages and head for the city. So no matter what arrived, more food, more supplies were still needed.

Colonel Mengistu had his own ideas on how to deal with his nation's catastrophe, which was now dominating headlines around the globe. He believed that if people were starving in the Ethiopian Highlands the solution was simple: shift the population to the Lowlands where there was food, land and water. It didn't matter that this was a completely different climatic zone to that which the farmers of Tigray were used to and one in which tropical diseases, to which the Tigrayans had no resistance, abounded. It was his solution and the peasants would go – whether they liked it or not. Staring down the barrel of an AK-47 if necessary. Mengistu was fighting a bitter war against Eritrean separatists and the TPLF in Tigray. He believed that the rebels were being aided by peasant farmers, likening the situation to that of fish swimming in the sea. 'Without the sea there will be no fish,' the despot claimed. 'We have to drain the sea, or if we cannot completely drain it, we must bring it to a level where they will lack room to move at will, and their movements will be easily restricted.'

In October 1984, the regime resettlement target was to move 300,000 families, about 1.5 million people, out of the mountainous north. Transit camps were set up in the Highlands to hold both those who had volunteered to go – and the many who had been coerced, often at gunpoint. In the course of 15 months, more than 500,000 people were herded onto Antonov cargo planes, lorries and buses to be resettled. Despite the promise of a better life, the plough animals, seed and fertilizers that were pledged often failed to materialize. To make matters worse, thousands of the refugees perished from disease, exacerbated by poor sanitation. The Tigrayans understood well that God's wrath brought famine but this transplanting of people – and the death that ensued – was, without any doubt, the work of man.

Woldu noticed the huge planes coming into land as he wandered among the hordes of starving after arriving back at Kwiha from the Latchi clinic. It was the third week of November. Clutching the hands of Birhan and Azmera, he desperately searched among the multitude before he finally found Letebirhan with Lemlem and Silas.

Robust Lemlem ran forward and clasped her father's bony leg. Letebirhan beamed down at her as she welcomed back her sisters. There were tears and prayers of gratitude. Letebirhan explained that food aid from the aircraft had come in their absence but that it was pitifully inadequate. More desperate farming families were arriving at Mekele all the time. There were huge queues at both the clinics and feeding stations. The lucky children were given a high-energy milk drink made from butter oil, dried skimmed milk, sugar and boiling water – rather like that given to Azmera.

Woldu had been given some money by a *farenji* in Latchi and was able to buy some barley to roast. The family were still sleeping in the open with just a couple of filthy shawls to keep out the biting mountain winds during the freezing nights. As the November of 1984 wore on, the couple developed a routine whereby Woldu, trying to make his little money last, searched for whatever scraps of food he could find from friends or food centre queues while Letebirhan looked after the four girls.

Birhan was still weak from her near-death illness but the three-year-old appeared to be almost her normal self as the family's chatterbox. She liked to play with one-year-old Silas, drawing pictures in the dust with twigs of stick donkeys and dogs. Lemlem, always strong, helped Letebirhan make a small fire to roast any grain the family managed to find. Five-year-old Azmera seemed more listless than the others and was desperately thin. She seemed unable to regain her strength.

The Hercules planes kept coming but it wasn't enough. Every day more people died.

Bob Geldof's anger hadn't dissipated in the month since the starving of Mekele had been seared into his conscience by the BBC coverage. As more reports reached the West from the famine zone, Geldof was busy assembling a stellar group of musicians. A press officer at Phonogram suggested the name 'Band Aid' for the group as a pun on the adhesive plaster placed on a wound along with its more literal meaning.

As more and more stars pledged their support to the project the media interest also became more intense. The tabloid newspaper the *Daily Mirror* ran a campaign to raise money for 'mercy flights' to Tigray while the appeal by my own paper *The Sun* raised £100,000. Geldof's drive and enthusiasm were relentless. He was painfully aware that Ethiopians were dying by the second and knew that the song he had created with Midge Ure, 'Do They Know It's Christmas?', needed to be in the shops soon to have any real effect.

Pop artist Peter Blake, who made the famous arrow and target Mod logo for British pop group The Who in the 1960s and created the cover of *Sergeant Pepper's Lonely Hearts Club Band* for The Beatles, designed a montage for the record's cover. It showed two emaciated Ethiopian children covered with flies amid scenes from a traditional Western Christmas of wrapped presents, fine food and drink and happy families.

Everything seemed set and Geldof and Ure were the first to arrive at SARM Studios in West London's Ladbroke Grove on Sunday, November 25. When former Genesis singer Phil Collins turned up expecting the band to be just George Michael, Sting, Bob Geldof, Midge Ure and himself on drums. He found instead a *Who's Who* of Pop.

Geldof remembers the assembly of the biggest stars in British chart music at the time looking like 'a bunch of yobs down the pub on a Sunday lunchtime'. Duran Duran had come back early from their tour of Germany, U2 had flown in from Dublin, Spandau Ballet were there, as were George Michael and Paul Weller, the former singer from The Jam. Boy George, one of the biggest stars of the 1980s, was supposed to be there but was still in New York where his band Culture Club had been touring. Geldof dialled his hotel room at 6am local time. *'George, it's Geldof, where the fuck are you?'* Soon Boy George was jetting across the Atlantic on Concorde.

The gathered vocalists were given their individual lines to sing and the egos of around 40 pop stars were put to one side, for a few hours at least. Boy George finally arrived from New

York at which Geldof yelled: 'Get on with it you old queen.' George hissed back: 'Shut up you Irish tart.'

The soloists were told their lines: Paul Young sang: *'It's Christmas time, there's no need to be afraid. At Christmas time, we let in light and we banish shade.'* And U2's Bono roared: *'Well, tonight thank God it's them instead of you.'*

Despite the worthiness of the cause, for some, the day still meant rock and roll excess. British rock band Status Quo's Francis Rossi and Rick Parfitt found themselves a corner of the studio to party, reportedly snorting line after line of cocaine.

Midge Ure, who produced the song, mixed it overnight and early the next morning it was on a bike to the pressing plant. 'Later Bob took a cassette round to Radio 1 where he said: "Life this year is a piece of plastic with a hole in the middle." We were hoping to sell around 100,000 copies and get the Christmas Number One.'

Geldof had used his persuasive enthusiasm to get British high-street retailers Woolworths, WH Smiths, HMV, Virgin, Boots and Our Price to waive their profits from selling the single. ICI donated the vinyl to make the records. Only the Value Added Tax (VAT) on the single prevented 100 percent of the sale price going to Ethiopia. Sensing the strength of public opinion Prime Minister Margaret Thatcher's government backed down, handing the tax money over to charity.

The mid-1980s was supposed to be an age of rampant capitalism and greed but 'Do They Know It's Christmas?' immediately caught the imagination of the public when it was released on November 29. Soon the record was flying off the shelves. Some people bought boxes of the single to send out as Christmas cards. Others walked into a shop, bought 50 copies, kept one and put the other 49 back.

A Plymouth butcher rang Geldof to ask if he needed special permission to sell records. When Geldof replied 'no' the meat was removed from the man's shop window and replaced by records. In London, the Queen's grocer Fortnum and Mason sold thousands in its restaurant.

The hastily recorded tune topped the charts in 13 countries, becoming the fastest-selling single of all time in the UK, with a million copies sold in the first week alone. It stayed at Number One for five weeks, selling over three million copies and becoming easily the then biggest-selling single of all time in the UK. It was later overtaken by Elton John's 'Candle in the Wind' in 1997, released in tribute to Diana, Princess of Wales, after her death.

In the United States, Band Aid sold 1.5 million copies in a fortnight. Geldof sounded out US artists such as Cyndi Lauper, The Cars and Hall and Oates about doing a US equivalent of Band Aid, stressing it was up to the American bands to organize it themselves.

'It was a phenomenon,' Geldof says. 'Not because it was a good record but because it was your membership card. It was saying, "I'm not going along with this. There's not much I can do. I don't know how to stop someone having to undergo this nightmare but I'm not party to this. I'm not complicit to this mass murder. I'm really not. How do you know? Because I'm buying this record. Fuck you." There was real rage and anger, it wasn't wishy-washy. What was pathetic is that the price of a life that year was a seven-inch piece of plastic.'

The record kept selling in subsequent years. The Band Aid Trust handed out £75 million to famine relief projects across Africa between January 1985 and November 2004. Geldof pledged to spend 20 percent of the money on emergency relief, 20 percent on logistics, and 60 percent on long-term development. Around £43 million was spent in the first year. Band Aid ships carried nearly 100,000 tonnes (98,420 tons) of food, shelter, medical equipment and vehicles to Africa in 18 months from April 1985. Fleets of Band Aid trucks hauled food from the Red Sea ports into Tigray; more lorries carried food across Sudan. There were long-term development projects building schools, health clinics and dams and planting trees.

Geldof's infectious can-do attitude had shown how individuals could circumvent governments and organizations to fight poverty. The simple act of buying a pop record could save a life. The rich First World had finally sat up and taken notice of what was happening in the Third. The outpouring of public sympathy forced Western governments to reverse their aid policies on Ethiopia. The US government sent 500,000 tonnes (492,100 tons) of grain. Britain sent food and committed another £50 million for aid. Geldof was canonized by sections of the media as 'Saint Bob'. Others lambasted him as being out of his depth in the aid world. Critics said that the name of the song itself, 'Do They Know It's Christmas?', was inappropriate in a nation so full of staunch Christians.

When Claire Berstchinger originally heard the song on her little short-wave radio curled up in her bed at the Castle Hotel on a rocky outcrop above the bustle of Mekele, she was horrified. 'The reception was really bad and I heard them singing, *"Feed the world, let them know it's Christmas time."* And I thought, "What are they talking about?" Getting completely the wrong end of the stick, I was incandescent with rage. Who was this Bob Geldof to capitalize on the misery of the displaced people of Ethiopia?" I thought everyone involved was taking a percentage and making a quick buck for themselves. Isolated in Mekele, I knew nothing of the extraordinary work he was doing.'

Michael Buerk was initially revolted by the idea, too. 'When I heard about the Band Aid record, I thought, "Who are these creeps?" I had the stereotypical view of rock singers as self-indulgent airheads lining their pockets. I went back to Ethiopia a fortnight after Christmas and there were about eight Hercules aircraft carrying aid on the ground where we'd flown in. It was impressive.'

In Ethiopia, Woldu and his family had absolutely no reason to celebrate. Help might be on its way but it was too late for their daughter, Azmera. Weak from hunger, she had fallen desperately ill. Even today Woldu finds it too difficult to discuss Azmera's last days but Letebirhan remembers the child returning with Birhan and their father from the Latchi clinic when she was still strong. A fortnight later, however, she could barely support herself on her stick-like legs. Malnourishment had left Azmera fatally weakened, her body unable to fight off the plethora of diseases sweeping across the plains – tuberculosis, typhoid, pneumonia, diarrhoea and flu. Her family believe that she came down with a 'fever'.

Letebirhan says: 'We had a few grains of barley that Woldu had bought with the money he got in Latchi and we were able to get some handouts of a milk energy drink but Azmera was too ill to eat. There were no doctors, no *farenjis* to help.'

Every night the family huddled together on the windswept plain and tried to drift off to sleep as the hyenas scavenged in the darkness. One morning when the family awoke they couldn't stir Azmera. 'She had slipped away from us,' Letebirhan murmurs. 'Woldu knelt down and held her body and wept and wept and wept.'

They buried Azmera at St Mary's with the help of local people who were paid to collect the bodies of the dead.

Woldu prayed: 'Please God, save the rest of my daughters. We weren't any different from all the other people falling like leaves on the plain. But we asked God to spare the rest of our daughters. We were terrified they would die too.' Woldu occasionally theorizes that Azmera was bitten by a snake – the biblical connotations of evil implicit in that idea. It is only when the family talk privately that Woldu really speaks about his feelings: 'Azmera was a beautiful, well-behaved and clever girl. I still miss her now with all my heart and wonder what she would have done in life. What her children would have looked like.'

Birhan doesn't remember those torturous final days of her big sister's short life. Her memories are of happier times, of playing games in the sunlight of their home village and of the long days when Azmera helped raise her spirits when she was convalescing by making Birhan's lips 'blubble' with her tiny fingers.

The transport aircraft laden with aid kept coming. Governments and non-governmental organizations (NGOs) had been propelled into action by the public outburst of humanitarianism with Band Aid as its catalyst. But the planes were too late for Azmera and for thousands of others who went to their graves that autumn. Although food was now arriving by the tonne, people were still hungry.

Among the consignments were more army-surplus-style canvas tents, which were erected in Kwiha, just a short walk up a rocky hillside from St Mary's on the way to the airstrip. Woldu and his surviving family were among the lucky ones offered a place to sleep. Finally they were able to get out of the bitter wind.

Woldu felt more secure now they had some shelter. His family was still desperately weak and hungry but food aid was finally getting through. Along with their neighbours, they joined the snaking queues of the needy hoping for milk powder, bread, rice or porridge. Birhan gulped down the high-calorie milk drink so quickly that it dribbled from the corners of her mouth and stained her cheeks, but the foreign aid helped keep her alive.

Always industrious, Woldu believed that if the rest of his young family were to survive the Great Famine he would need to support them himself. He hated relying on charity; he was – and remains – a proud man. He was also terrified that the aid might disappear as suddenly as it had come. What would happen then? How would they survive? So he decided to forage for firewood to sell as cooking fuel. For that he would need a donkey as a pack animal to carry the bundles of thorny branches down the slopes of the wild mountains. It was close to Christmas Day of 1984 and with the last of the birr he got from the *farenji* in Latchi, he set off at dawn for the village of Monous some 10km (6 miles) away, where he knew friends who would sell him an animal.

Woldu hugged his girls and Letebirhan tightly, then set off in his deceptive lolloping gait at what was more a running than walking pace. Knowing every goat path in the tinder-dry mountains, he was nearing the little village of *sekela*-thatched huts when a khaki-clad figure stepped from behind the acacia brush surrounding the track and blocked his way.

When Woldu remonstrated with him, the soldier simply raised his Kalashnikov. As Woldu begged for mercy another soldier arrived, then another. They were Mengistu's men – government troops. Woldu was herded at gunpoint to Monous village where an army unit had encircled dozens of frightened villagers, mostly men. Woldu slumped down, waves of desperation sweeping over him. He was terrified that he would never see Letebirhan or his daughters again. How would his family survive? What would they eat now? He wondered if he could he make a run for it without being shot.

A Derg officer began to bark out orders. The group was told to get to its feet. The villagers were surrounded by men in uniform. They were shepherded onto a bus and driven to a holding camp near Mekele's ramshackle airstrip. If anyone tried to escape, the soldiers immediately opened fire on them. Woldu remembers hearing shots throughout the night. Armed soldiers even accompanied villagers to the latrines to prevent them from running away. Woldu was given a single bread roll to eat each day. He and hundreds of others were forced to sleep in the open on the bare, cold earth. It was here that he eventually spent Christmas Day. 'I was alone and desperately worried for my family,' he recalls.

In the tents at Kwiha, Letebirhan was terrified after Woldu failed to return from his trip to buy the donkey. He had taken the few birr that the family had left. She was left with three hungry children to look after alone. They had to hope they were lucky enough to receive the Western food aid that was being distributed. Christmas Day came and went without mother and daughters registering it.

Letebirhan says: 'It could have been Epiphany, Easter, Monday or Tuesday. It could have been day or night. We were so hungry we couldn't think. The only thing that was in our heads was who was going to die next.'

Geldof's lyrics, scorned by some, were presciently true. The people of Ethiopia were really too hungry – and they didn't know or care that it was Christmas.

Geldof, on his first visit to Africa, was in Ethiopia that Christmas. He was on a fact-finding mission to assess how to spend the £8 million that the 'Do They Know It's Christmas?' single had raised so far. As Band Aid became a global phenomenon, he had immersed himself in the intricacies of the aid business and Third World geopolitics.

The children's fund UNICEF had sent its resident representative in Addis to London to brief the singer on the situation on the ground in Ethiopia. Geldof, after much thought, made the decision that as the millions that were flooding in from the sale of the single were coming in from all over the world, no single agency from any one nation would have access to the whole pot. He also wanted to bypass agencies that would take some of the cash to meet their overheads. But the question was how should the money be spent most effectively? He concluded that the best way to find out how to spend the money was to make a personal visit to Ethiopia's famine-hit regions and see what was happening first hand.

He agreed to let British tabloids the *Daily Star* and *Daily Express* pay for his hotel bills while the British breakfast television station TV-am would pay for his flights. He didn't want to use any of the Band Aid funds for such purposes. He made it clear though that there would be no exclusives and no pictures of him posing with starving children.

Geldof arrived in Addis from London with a planeload of journalists in tow on Christmas Eve in the Ethiopian calendar (January 6 in the West). He was greeted by Berhane Deressa, Deputy Commissioner of the Ethiopian government's Relief and Rehabilitation Commission (RRC). On a whistle-stop tour of the capital, the pair passed through the concrete Arch of the Revolution with its huge hammer and sickle and the words *Long Live Proletarian Revolution*'.

Staring at it, Geldof turned to Deressa and said in his usual candid manner: 'Christ! No wonder there's a famine here if you insist on putting up crap like that. In any case, it's palpably not true. If there was any proletarian internationalism you wouldn't have millions dying here.'

Deressa suggested that Geldof spend Christmas in the holy Christian city of Lalibela in the north, where the churches are hewn from the surrounding rock and are viewed as a wonder of the world. Geldof wanted to go to the feeding camps in that area anyway. He boarded a battered DC-9 to Lalibela, where he was taken to a nearby feeding centre. He remembers a woman carrying her baby suffering from marasmus, severe protein-energy malnutrition that made the child look like 'a little monkey'. It wasn't the people's appearance that upset Geldof most though. It was their glazed and blank eyes. They were the eyes, he said, of people who had given up. Geldof wept even though he knew that 'crying was useless and a waste of energy'.

Geldof and his entourage then flew 300km (186 miles) north to Mekele. They were led to the tented area around a feeding camp run by several organizations, including the Red Cross. Somewhere among the multitude on that arid plain were Birhan and her family clinging desperately to life. There were still thousands of people without shelter. Geldof remembers huge huts of corrugated iron with concrete floors packed with people. 'It reminded me of the films I had seen on Auschwitz. There were 50,000 people here and more arriving every day. This place was hot too, and the tents buzzed with flies and disease.' Birhan and her sister went unnoticed among the heaving crowd.

He returned to Addis where the Christian Relief and Development Association, an umbrella organization coordinating NGOs like Save the Children, Oxfam and dozens of others, was to draw up suggestions about how the Band Aid money should be spent.

As Geldof swept through Mekele, Woldu was still being detained in the Derg's holding camp. The soldiers again refused to tell him why he was being held, of what crime he was being accused. He pleaded with them to let him contact his wife and children, who were in nearby Kwiha, as they didn't even know he was alive, but to no avail. Instead, he watched as some of the people were herded out of the camp, away towards the airstrip. They didn't come back. Soon there was enough room for him to sleep in one of the stone outbuildings to escape the night chill.

After two weeks of continual pleading with the soldiers, Woldu was given the go-ahead by an officer to look for his family. Three armed soldiers hustled him into a battered green jeep and he directed them onto the main road out of Mekele towards Kwiha. He wasn't sure what he would find.

He was relieved to find them where he had left them in the big canvas tent near the ramshackle stone huts of the little market town. They were still alive. He strode towards Letebirhan and his daughters, weaving in and out of the sick and the starving. He hugged little Birhan and Lemlem, who both stood up to wrap their arms around his legs. The men with guns, however, were still close behind. They were waiting to round up the family.

Letebirhan still shudders at the memory. 'The children cowered behind me. The soldiers shouted, "Hurry up. Hurry up." I can still see their faces. They were so angry. We were then loaded into a big truck with many other families who had been taken too. We were terrified. People were getting separated from their children. We just made sure we held onto ours. The children weren't crying; they didn't have a clue what was going on. We were prisoners. The Derg men were armed with guns. We had no choice but to follow their orders.'

They were taken back to the camp where Woldu had been held. That night they slept on the bare soil. There was no breakfast, and lunch and dinner were both just two small bread rolls. For a week they watched the big planes landing on the airstrip. Many were huge Antonov cargo planes.

'The soldiers were taking people away from the camp,' Woldu says. 'We had no idea where they were going, but they were taking them by force.

'Then one morning they came for us.'

A Derg soldier motioned with his rifle for Woldu and his family and dozens of other bedraggled peasants to get to their feet. They were then forced onto a green army lorry and driven to the airport. Woldu still didn't know why they had been detained in the first place.

At Mekele's airstrip, ringed by the tinder-dry mountains, they discovered a huge Antonov cargo plane waiting; its rear doors gaping open like a shark's jaws. The blades of the engine were ticking over. To the Tigrayans, used to travelling by donkey, it must have presented a terrifying sight. They were herded like cattle into its depths.

Woldu had his hands full with Birhan and baby Silas. Lemlem, along with Letebirhan, limping as quickly as her damaged leg would allow, pushed into the Antonov's hold and found a small patch of floor space for them to huddle in.

The huge rear door began to slowly close, the interior now a barely lit murk. The engines roared and the plane took off, taking them to God only knew where.

THE LONG
WALK HOME

EXODUS

THE RUSSIAN ANTONOV'S straining engines broke through the seam of thick cloud enveloping the barren mountains around Mekele, causing the labouring aircraft to bump and flounder. Inside the plane's cavernous hold there was turmoil. Packed in like cattle, the dozens of Tigrayan families, dressed in little more than filthy rags, were in distress; most had never travelled in a car before, let alone an aircraft. High-pitched wails now drowned out the words of those intoning their prayers in the glow provided by small interior lights attached to the fuselage.

Woldu was holding on tight to Birhan and Lemlem, while Letebirhan held baby Silas. They perched on a patch of floor space; there were no seats and they rattled around the plane. Other people tried to get to their feet, terrified by the pitching of the aircraft, unsettled by the turbulence outside, only to topple over moments later, crushing those on the floor beneath them. This caused more panic. Those desperate to go to the toilet or sick with diarrhoea simply went where they sat. Woldu recalls: 'We were crushed in together. There were screams – there was sick everywhere. We had no idea how this thing had got in the air; it was like a miracle to us.

'When the plane went up our hearts were in our stomachs. Children were crying in terror; it was chaos. But Birhan and Lemlem sat quietly.'

Woldu was resigned to their fate. After witnessing the death of both Azmera and Alemetsehay, he trusted his remaining family's destiny to God. 'I wasn't scared anymore. I had seen children dying and their parents crying. I had witnessed hell… I could cry no more.'

After a jarring flight of more than two hours, the Antonov plunged back towards earth, touching down at an airstrip in Nekemte, a bustling market town in western Ethiopia around 1,300km (800 miles) away from Mekele by road, where the Oromo are the dominant people; they have their own distinct language and culture. For the Tigrayan Highlanders, this may as well have been the other end of the Earth, so alien was it to them. The terrified Tigrayan villagers were loaded onto four old buses, usually used by the military to transport troops. A Derg soldier told Woldu and the other farmers that they were lucky, that the famine was over for them. He informed them that they were being taken to a place where 'the rivers flowed deep and the corn grew strong and green', but all Woldu could think was how far he was from his beloved homeland.

The column of buses trundled westwards through lush meadows and dense fig groves towards the Sudanese border. The blazing sun and the muggy humidity saw temperatures over 35°C (95°F), but as the buses descended the Highland plateau towards Gambela in the Lowlands, the Tigrayans kept the bus windows firmly closed. The mountain people are superstitious; they believe that the wind spreads disease and after so much loss, the people aboard the bus could not bear to see more deaths among their already depleted masses.

Peering through the dirty glass window, Woldu saw lyre-horned cattle with humped backs wandering in knots through marshy reed beds in the valley bottoms. He recalls thinking how well the cattle looked in comparison to the starving herds in the north. Monkeys chattered in the tree tops and widowbirds with their long black tail feathers and yellow shoulders flitted through dense thickets of elephant grass. Wild mango, papaya and banana flourished on the fertile land here.

He was captivated by the strange plant and birdlife. For the past few months they had seen little but carrion-eating vultures, waiting silently for death to bring their next meal. Here, huge white-billed and bald-headed marabou storks patrolled the river banks and brilliantly plumed grebes, herons, and ibises flapped from the marshy valley bottoms as they passed. After such a long period of drought and famine the family gazed at the clear, running water with wonder. Woldu was desperate to immerse himself in it, to wash the dirt away.

The soldiers handed out cups of boiled wheat to the starving group as the vehicles trundled slowly through the fertile meadows and luxuriant river valleys. 'It was so green; it looked perfect farming land,' Woldu recalls.

The buses snaked over the slow-flowing Didesa River, a tributary of the mighty Blue Nile, the banks of which were thick with bamboo and elephant grass. They continued west past the small town of corrugated tin shacks at Gimbi close to where they stopped for the night. The Tigrayans slept in their seats on the buses, fearful of their unfamiliar surroundings and of what might lie ahead of them.

The next day the buses started up again and they continued along potholed dirt roads through gentle hills covered in yellow fields of the native grain *tef*. After travelling for some hours the buses finally shuddered to a halt. Woldu remembers a thick jungle of deep-green evergreen trees falling away to a broad, sweeping valley of rich grassland and acacia scrub. He could hear the sound of running water nearby and grizzled-grey vervet monkeys shrieking in the trees overhead. Coffee plants grew wild beneath a canopy of ancient, vine-tangled trees.

A Derg soldier shouted: 'Get out! Your people are here.'

He pointed into the thick forest: 'Go and find your people.'

Woldu and his family and hundreds of other Tigrayan farmers had been relocated to a resettlement camp as part of Mengistu's policy to prevent starvation among his people. There were similar new villages of resettled mountain people dotted across the Lowlands. By February 1986, when the resettlement campaign was stopped, around 600,000 people had been moved; an estimated 50,000 had died in the upheaval.

Woldu and the girls were given a tiny, stone-walled hut with grass thatch woven onto eucalyptus boughs and a scrap of land to plough. Even today, the family is unsure of the exact location of that village but it was around 150km (90 miles) west of Nekemte and some 100km (60 miles) from the border with Sudan.

The Derg authorities promised food until the Tigrayans' first harvest. They would get grain to plant and would share ploughs and beehives, as well as pots and pans, with their new neighbours who, though Tigrayans, were still strangers.

It was the time of the Orthodox festival of Timkat (Epiphany), celebrated on January 19 in the Western calendar. It is the most important feast day in the Orthodox year and a time of celebration, commemorating the Baptism of Jesus in the Jordan River. A priest blesses a nearby body of water towards dawn and then members of the congregation enter the water and immerse themselves, symbolically renewing their baptismal vows. *Tej* and *tella* – Ethiopian mead and beer – are brewed and special bread is baked, while the fat-tailed African sheep are slaughtered for a sumptuous meal. It is a time when gifts are bought or made for children and new clothes purchased or old ones mended and laundered. For Woldu and his family – and all the people who had travelled so far with him – there were no lambs to slaughter, no gifts, no new clothes, no feast. Instead they were trying to start a farm from scratch, to till the virgin soil before the spring rains came. Their new village was squalid, with clogged, stinking latrines filled with raw sewage close to the area where the children played. Malaria-carrying mosquitoes hovered over the fetid pools.

Their new fields were, the government authorities told them, unoccupied land. Yet, when Birhan and Lemlem took some old yellow plastic containers to the river for water soon after they arrived they met some Lowlanders. The Anuwak fishermen – who believe that if you keep walking you will fall off the end of the world – and Nuer pastoralists are the ethnic groups which predominate in the area.

Looking back at that time Birhan says, 'There were darker-skinned people there who were naked with big knives. They were different from us but friendly to us little ones.'

It was clearly apparent that the Tigrayan newcomers would be competing for land for pasture with local people. Woldu borrowed a plough ox from some other resettled Tigrayans and then, in the stifling tropical heat, sowed a small patch of land with wheat. He then waited – waited and prayed for rain. Without it they would have nothing and until then the family was dependent on handouts of grain from the authorities and the goodwill of a strange people, whose land they seemed to have been forced to take. The future seemed very uncertain. Only Woldu's faith could keep him going.

Some 6,000km (3,700 miles) away musician Bob Geldof could have decided that he had done enough for Africa after the unprecedented and unparalleled success of 'Do They Know It's Christmas?' The song had raised millions for immediate relief aid for the hungry and focused the world's attention and, in particular, that of the heads of international governments, on Ethiopia and the famine and war raging there. It also empowered and politicized a generation to become activists and fund-raisers in its own right.

Geldof took his band The Boomtown Rats on a packed sell-out tour of Britain in early 1985. There, he experienced what he would later refer to as the 'God syndrome' for the first time. Audience members would come up to him after the gig, in his words, 'moist-eyed, touching you and looking at you' as if he'd descended from heaven. Geldof, however, gave anyone wishing to deify him short shrift.

'I told them to "Fuck off!"', he says bluntly.

Buckets, shaken at every gig, raised a further £50,000 for Band Aid, but the success of the shows did little for The Rats' record sales. In the meantime, Geldof received a telephone call from an American pop manager called Ken Kragen who had got together with the African American singer, actor and social activist Harry Belafonte to create a US equivalent to the British-based Band Aid. Belafonte had seen Geldof on TV promoting 'Do They Know It's Christmas?' and stated that as a black man looking at Africans suffering he was 'ashamed and embarrassed at seeing a bunch of white English kids doing what black Americans ought to have been doing.'

Geldof travelled to Los Angeles in January 1985 for the recording of the single 'We Are The World', the song that had been written by two of the world's greatest living black artists of that time, Michael Jackson, then at the height of his career, and former Commodores' singer Lionel Richie. Unlike the British recording of 'Do They Know It's Christmas?', which was comparatively relaxed with one man on the door and food from a local takeaway, this was a glitzy Hollywood occasion. There were security guards, special admittance passes to the studio, canapés and caviar, albeit donated free.

'We Are The World' was recorded by a truly stellar cast of musicians: pretty much every big name in music had turned out to be part of the group collectively called 'USA For Africa'. It included Bob Dylan, Ray Charles, Diana Ross, Stevie Wonder, Tina Turner, Paul Simon, Bruce Springsteen and Dionne Warwick. On arrival the stars were greeted by a sign pinned to the studio door, which read: 'Please check your egos at the door'. Ken Kragen gave Geldof, fresh from his visit to Ethiopia, a chance to speak to the gathered superstars before recording started.

'I think what's happening in Africa is a crime of historic proportions,' he railed. 'You walk into one of the corrugated iron huts and you see meningitis and malaria and typhoid buzzing around the air. And you see dead bodies lying side by side with the live ones. In some of the camps you see 15 bags of flour for 27,000 people. And I assume that's why we're all here tonight.'

On March 7, 1985, 'We Are The World' was released. At that time, Birhan and her family and thousands of others were trying to eke out life in the resettlement camps. It would shift an incredible 20 million copies. As well as topping the US chart, the single reached Number One in the UK, France, New Zealand, The Netherlands, Norway, Sweden and Switzerland. Band Aid had gone global.

In Canada, Brian Stewart's groundbreaking reports from Tigray – which included the agonizing shots of Birhan seconds away from death – had prompted pop manager Bruce Allen to bring together Canada's biggest stars to record 'Tears Are Not Enough' under the band name Northern Lights. International artists performing on the record included Bryan Adams, Joni

Mitchell, Neil Young and Paul Anka. The song's video opens with footage from Stewart's original CBC News report on the famine, and then cuts to the performers singing the song in a studio. It raised millions to help alleviate the suffering the journalist had so vividly captured on film. All-in-all there were around 25 Band Aid-type records for Africa repeated around the world. Birhan and her family still knew nothing of Band Aid or Bob Geldof. Indeed they had never seen a TV or listened to a radio. Nor could they read or write.

Despite sparking this global outpouring of compassion and goodwill, Bob Geldof still wasn't satisfied. He had had another idea: he wanted to stage a concert. 'I knew that there were 22 million people starving to death in Africa and that £8 million was enough to keep them alive for two weeks,' Geldof later wrote in his memoirs *Is That It?* 'The point of the record had been to raise money but, more important, to raise issues and make a gesture.'

Geldof gave himself 20 weeks to organize a gig of the world's biggest stars in two parts – one in London and one in Philadelphia. He decided to call it Live Aid. It was to become the biggest fund-raising event, the biggest TV event and the biggest concert that the world, up until then, had ever seen.

Woldu cannot remember the name the Derg gave the new settlement of little stone houses built for them by the Lowlanders where the family were forced to stay, but the land here was fertile, crops were growing. And they were alive. The corn that Woldu had sown was growing strong and luxuriantly green. Families, many desperately malnourished, survived for the time being on meagre food handouts. They had little in the way of cooking utensils and farming tools. 'We were given one cooking pan for every seven households,' Leterbirhan comments quietly. 'You had to queue up to use it.'

The sanitation drainage system was completely inadequate; the houses had been built far too close together. The Highlanders, unused to the dank heat of the Lowland valley, began to fall prey to disease during the spring months of 1985. Then there was an outbreak of deadly cholera.

'It was such an unhealthy place,' Woldu exclaims. 'There were people there from all over the country and they brought diseases with them. When the cholera came people were dying like flies. Death was all around us again. I swore I wouldn't let my daughters die there, in the Lowlands where we didn't belong. If we were destined to die then it would be in our mountains, in our beautiful village of Lahama.'

More people were being resettled in the village all the time. Then one day Woldu's neighbours' five-year-old little girl was struck down with a terrible malady. They could hear her rasping, cough throughout the balmy night, which gradually became a death rattle; then the coughing stopped, only to be replaced with the sound of the weeping of her parents. The little girl was the same age as Woldu's daughter Azmera had been when she had died. While Woldu grieved for the parents, knowing what they were going through, he could only thank God he still had Lemlem, Birhan and Silas.

After four months in the now disease-ridden Lowlands Woldu made the momentous decision to leave, to take his family back to their ancestral mountains. He still had around 100 birr – about £4 or US $6 – from the *farenji* in Latchi hidden in his tunic, with which he could buy scraps of food.

One of the immediate problems was how to leave. The local buses had been told not to pick up Tigrayans by the authorities who were worried that the people they had forcibly resettled would abscond back to their homelands. Letebirhan's hair, braided in traditional Highland cornrows on her scalp, combined with the fact that they spoke Tigrinya, would give them away. But they didn't have much choice anyway, Woldu decided. They didn't have enough money to pay for the bus fares, which would be around 300 birr each back to Mekele and as for plane tickets… They would simply have to make the journey by foot.

'I had seen so much death in my life,' says Woldu. 'Now I knew we had to run to save our lives. Everything was awful in the Lowlands. I had no idea how far it was back to Lahama but I knew we must go. If I had known how far it really was, I don't think I would have attempted it.'

The journey was an epic one. They would have to follow the main arterial road to Nekemte, pass through Addis Ababa before heading north to Mekele and Lahama. It was at least 470km (290 miles) to Addis; then around a further 800km (500 miles) back to Lahama. The family would also be fugitives and armed Derg patrols were roaming the countryside looking for resettled people attempting to return to their homeland. They were far from the only ones attempting to flee home. Thousands were trying to escape the resettlement camps despite the risk of being shot.

At first light, Woldu and his young family made ready to go. Woldu strapped a 6.6kg (14.4lb) sack of roasted wheat into a *kuta* – a small shawl – and tied it around his waist. Also strapped to his body were blankets, ox skins, a sickle for cutting wild plants and a small cooking pan.

As they started heading east, Woldu glanced back at Letebirhan. Barefoot, her pronounced limp gave her a laboured, rolling gait. Although Woldu knew she was a tough woman, used to working hard in the fields and walking for 10 hours to market and back, he was still worried for her. She was a good and loving wife and had taken care of his girls as if they were her own.

'Woldu was determined we would get back to Tigray,' Letebirhan recalls. 'The Lowlands were so green but so many people were dying. So, we started walking. I had no idea how far it would be, it was just walk, walk, walk all the time. We were told by people at a food distribution point that it would be like being born again, it was so far. Woldu is small but he is a very strong man and was able to carry his daughters. He would do anything for his family.'

Lemlem was a strong walker for an eight year old; she could follow her father's footsteps. Woldu, already laden down, placed little Silas on one shoulder, asking her to grip tightly to his neck, then he hoisted Birhan onto the other.

They walked due east, with the bright orange sun shining in their faces, towards Nekemte. Keeping off the main highway to avoid Derg patrols, they walked across rolling hills with panoramic views of goat herds grazing the pastures under eucalyptus groves. Fields of wheat and barley grew abundantly in the river basins.

'Every day we walked from sunrise to darkness,' Woldu says. 'At daybreak we would each eat a handful of roasted wheat and then have another at 3pm. I would cut wild herbs with my sickle, which we would have as salad. We all had the same food. I would ask villagers for fire on the route to roast our grain with and sometimes we would buy a little bread. Occasionally we paid 50 cents to stay with a family. They would give us sacks to sleep under, otherwise we would sleep on the ox skins under the stars. As we walked the girls held my neck tightly. They were so good; there were no tears.'

Birhan had slowly grown stronger since her brush with death on the plains of Mekele. She remembers well clinging to her father.

'He would call to me and say, "Are you alright Birhan?" Then I would nestle my face into his neck to let him know I

123

was fine. Silas was a baby and I would try and teach her some words as we moved along.'

After walking for over a week they saw the glint of the sun on the corrugated iron roofs of the shacks on the outskirts of Nekemte. They had covered around 150km (90 miles). The family slept on the fringes of the town in a ditch hidden from the road by dense elephant grass. In the morning they struck out east once more after asking the direction to Addis Ababa, some 322 km (200 miles) distant.

As they walked day after day towards the capital Birhan remembers being particularly terrified as they crossed a sharp precipice, which fell away to a gorge of jagged rocks hundreds of metres below. 'Silas and I would say: "Father, father, father, we don't want to fall down the cliff!" He would reassure us: "Don't worry my daughters, don't worry!" He encouraged us all the time; he had amazing strength.'

Woldu put his fate in the hands of the Lord. 'Our faith kept us going. God gave me strength. We saw other Tigrayans walking home but it was mostly bachelors – not families. The girls were so strong, they never complained. They were only worried when we walked along the cliffs; otherwise they were mostly quiet. They were good girls.'

Letebirhan was now struggling, however. 'I looked down at my feet and they were all bloody and blistered. Woldu had sandals made of rubber tyre, but I didn't have any shoes. I admit I cried. Every time we slept somewhere I said to Woldu: "This is it. I can't go on any further."'

Woldu says: 'I had to keep convincing Letebirhan to keep going. She cried often. We had to go slowly. I had to encourage her every step of the way. I never gave her anything to carry. We kept going on and on. We had no choice.'

They crossed rushing streams and broad valleys heading in the direction of the rising sun and the capital, which locals said was not far away now. Then disaster struck. Woldu awoke one morning in a glade of fig trees where the family had spent the night feeling deathly sick. Soon he was vomiting violently. He retreated behind a bush a few metres away from the family as he began suffering from diarrhoea. He was determined to go on though, knowing his family's lives lay in his hands, he knew they couldn't stay where they were at the roadside. Somehow he got to his feet, hoisted his daughters on to his shoulders, and strode on.

During that dreadful journey, he had to stop several more times, stricken with violent stomach spasms as the diarrhoea made it impossible for him to keep walking. He went to the toilet in the open, finding cover behind trees or in ditches where he could. When he felt slightly better he forced himself and the girls to go on. Anytime they came across running water he rehydrated himself, lapping up the water from the palms of his hands.

Soon they could see the pall of woodsmoke and car fumes in the defile below Mount Entoto, where Addis sprawled. They had now walked 470km (290 miles) from the resettlement camp and it had taken about four weeks.

Founded in 1886 by Emperor Menelik II, Addis Ababa – which means 'new flower' in Amharic – was now the crucible of Derg power. The exhausted and hungry family knew the danger they were in. Dressed in their tattered white *gabi* shawls and speaking the language of the rebel Tigray north, they were pretty much sitting ducks for the Derg. Woldu was now desperately weak and needed to rest and the family had to wait until nightfall before tentatively making their way into the teeming city.

The Addis of 1985 was a buzzing metropolis, populated by almost 1.5 million (it is more than double that size today). It was beyond anything the family had ever experienced before.

Blue and white-liveried Lada taxis honked their tinny horns as they dodged military convoys in streets lined with wooden street shacks selling biscuits, soap and matches. There were battered minibuses, donkey carts, bleating goats, herds of humpbacked cows and a mass of people coming and going. Beggars with missing limbs or bodies crippled by childhood polio begged for alms. As he passed the mud-walled shanty settlements on the outskirts of the city, Woldu could see the staring eyes of people in the glow of wood fires. He remained alert, conscious that they were in grave danger.

Suddenly a voice whispered urgently to them from the darkness: '*Quickly! Come here! Come inside!*' Knowing that he was taking a risk, but recognizing that he had little option, Woldu made his way towards the walled compound where the voice seemed to be coming from. A woman stood there. She was in her 30s and she spoke to them in Amharic. She said her name was Tigist. She gestured them inside, leading them through wrought-iron gates into a dusty little courtyard surrounding what to the weary travellers seemed like a palace, but was in fact a modest bungalow.

Woldu could hear the laughter of children playing inside. For the first time in a very long time, he began to relax. He crouched on his haunches so that Birhan and Silas could clamber down off his shoulders. Then he laid down his ox skins.

Shivering under the blanket draped around him, it suddenly struck him just how weary he was.

Despite his best efforts, he couldn't stop himself from drifting into a deep, deep sleep.

He was startled from his slumbers the next morning by the sound of a hectoring voice blaring from a loudspeaker. Peering through a crack in the gates, he saw a khaki-coloured army jeep outside on which the Derg had mounted amplifiers. A series of favoured slogans were shouted like '*Land to the Tiller*' before Woldu heard: '*If anyone takes in resettlement people, their homes will be seized and they will be punished.*'

Woldu was in despair. He recognized that he was too ill to continue the journey. He could barely walk, let alone carry his girls and all their possessions. It was clear their good Samaritan, Tigist, and her family could lose everything if they continued to let them stay. Letebirhan adds: 'It was very kind of this woman to take us in. It was a brave thing to do. She put her family at great risk.'

Tigist gave them their first decent meal in weeks, consisting of gristly *tibbs* goat meat sautéed in hot fat, which they greedily mopped up with rubbery *injera* bread. Meanwhile Woldu continued to suffer. He now thinks that he was suffering from cholera as he lay in Tigist's compound. 'I was very sick and couldn't get up, I couldn't move. I had a deep fever. I was praying to God to keep me alive. I was terrified my children would be eaten by hyenas on the way back to Tigray if I died.'

When he was able to, he gulped down as much fresh water as he could to rehydrate himself. He knew his body craved fluids lost during the severe bout of diarrhoea that had struck him during his long walk through the Lowlands.

The children were thriving, though, but were bored with being cooped up in the house. Lemlem, Birhan and Silas were soon running around the compound with Tigist's clutch of children playing hide-and-seek. Although it warmed Letebirhan's heart, she scolded them when they dashed through the iron gates out onto the streets. It was dangerous but it was too late. Some neighbours had seen them. Tigist was forced to go next door and beg: 'Please don't tell anyone these people are staying here. They are a good family.'

After five days of lying and barely moving in Tigist's Addis courtyard Woldu began to regain his strength. He knew that they had to move on. Their luck could only last so long. One of Tigist's neighbours could soon inform on them and they had already put the family in enough danger.

Finally he was able to raise himself from the ox skins. He asked Tigist to buy a small sack of wheat for their journey. They washed their tattered clothes and then gathered up their meagre possessions, the blankets to protect them from heat and cold, the ox skins, their cooking pan and sickle. Early on the morning of their sixth day in the compound, with the sun still below the horizon, Woldu crouched down to let Birhan and Silas clamber back onto his shoulders. Saying goodbye to Tigist and owing her more thanks than he could possibly ever repay, Woldu set off once more on his epic journey with his family in tow.

This time they walked north on the main trunk road that led to Mekele some 780km (480 miles) away through Tigray's tabletop mountains in the Ethiopian Highlands range. They started through the gloom on the road to Dessie.

'We had washed our clothes in Addis but we still stood out,' Woldu says. 'I was terrified people would still see we were from Tigray – resettlement people – and turn us in.'

As the unforgiving African sun beat down on them, they strode along the roadside trying to remain out of eyeshot of passing drivers. They passed friendly goatherds taking their animals to market in Addis who pointed them in the direction north through eucalyptus plantations clinging to the side of towering, volcanic mountains. The vegetation was lush in places, sometimes with rolling brown and green hills. They tried to walk away from the asphalted highway to avoid military patrols.

The family walked for around 20km (12 miles) from dawn until dusk before camping down amid a rock-strewn gorge carpeted with thick grass cropped short by goats. Woldu went to a nearby hut and asked a farming family for some wood then carefully roasted their wheat over a fire.

The next morning they set off early. Within a few minutes the family were forced to walk along the tarmacked main road by a plunging cliff that blocked their way. In a few minutes a white pickup truck drew up beside them. Woldu's heart sank. Was it a Derg sympathizer? Could it possibly be over just like that? Then, the middle-aged man behind the wheel began speaking to them urgently in Tigrinya. He muttered, 'There are Derg men everywhere – it is very dangerous for you.'

Woldu begged him for help, saying they were desperate to reach Tigray. Even though the driver was obviously terrified, he agreed. He ordered them to get into the back of the pickup and to hide under the blankets. Woldu and Letebirhan pulled the girls close to them as they were jolted along the bumpy highway. Later Woldu would feel the truck straining as it began climbing up the twisty road to the village of Tarmabir at 3,250 metres (10,662 feet) above sea level in the Amhara region.

And then he could smell the evergreen needles of the 20 metre- (66 feet) high African juniper trees and the air became crisper and colder. The pickup passed through a 587 metre- (1,926 feet) long, 8 metre- (26 feet) wide tunnel built by the occupying Italians so many years before. Gelada baboons frequent the forests near the tunnel.

The driver stopped in the village of Debre Sina and bought some biscuits and bananas. When he reached a quiet lay-by further along the road on a high heather-topped plateau he stopped and handed the food over to Woldu to give to his family, before he drove on. After nearly six hours on the road and with darkness falling the driver finally pulled over. The family could see the lights of Dessie a couple of kilometres in the distance. The driver explained that this was as far as he could take them. It was around 385km (240 miles) from where he had picked them up and they were now 2,600 metres (8,530 feet) high, near the base of Mount Tossa. Woldu thanked the driver profusely and blessed him as he pulled away. Afterwards he realized that he hadn't even asked the Good Samaritan's name.

The family clambered down the sandy roadside bank to try to find a sheltered place among the scrubland where they could spend the rest of the night. Woldu had no idea where he was but the driver had told him Mekele was around another 380km (226 miles) north. The family were used to being on the road by now. Lemlem, Birhan and Silas weren't afraid any more of the pitch darkness. They said their prayers, after eating some bread, and then all cuddled up together on the black and white ox skin.

At first light Woldu heaved his two daughters onto his severely aching shoulders – resilient Lemlem and Letebirhan still following on without complaint, even though the latter's bad leg was aching at the hip and knee.

'We walked and walked,' Birhan recalls. 'It seemed to go on forever. I was so hungry and tired. My father was encouraging us all the way. Silas and I would sometimes laugh together but most of the time we just stared at the mountains and the rivers.'

The Highland air of the Amhara region was cool and thin, so different from the intense tropical heat of the Lowlands. The people the family came across were kind, giving the family food and even donating some birr, but it was still hard going. After seven long days the family trudged into Weldiya, around 120km (75 miles) north from Dessie. It was now May 1985, over six weeks since they had left the Lowlands, and they still had a further 280km (175 miles) to go before they reached Mekele.

Woldu was getting increasingly tired as the days dragged on and the group's pace was slowing down, but they doggedly soldiered on, shadowing the snaking main road north – their ancestral home of Lahama ever present in their minds.

The smells and sights of the high mountains gradually became more familiar. The air was fresh and clear, scented by eucalyptus, the sky cloudless and a vivid deep blue. Black and white hornbills nested in the fissures in the cliffs and birds of prey soared on the alpine thermals. They were back in their beloved Tigray.

Now desperately fatigued, Woldu tried to ignore the ache in his shoulders from carrying his precious daughters such a distance. The soles of Letebirhan's feet were a mass of painful sores and calluses. The family skirted around the town of Alamata – home of a large Derg garrison – before making for Korem, where journalist Michael Buerk had filmed the first of his landmark reports the previous year. Unbeknown to Woldu, Western aid had poured into the region in the ensuing months.

The family walked on, making their way through plunging ravines and climbing high mountain passes. They headed towards Maychew, a staging-post town full of small hotels and bars, little shops and garages on the main road north from Mekele. It had taken them around a fortnight to reach this point from Dessie and two months in total from the disease-ridden Lowlands. Mekele was now just 80km (50 miles) away. Woldu, Letebirhan and the girls finally started to believe that Lahama was within reach. They were really going to make it home.

On they trudged.

It was now late June 1985. It looked as if, against all the odds, their epic walk might be successful. Negotiating a sharp hairpin in the road close to Maychew, they began to talk of home. Of the prickly pear cactus fruit that flourished in Lahama and other familiar things. At last they dared hope.

They followed the bend in the road only to find themselves suddenly facing a group of men, dressed in green and armed with

Kalashnikovs. Woldu's heart raced as he quietly told his family to remain calm. They had stumbled upon a Derg checkpoint. Running away was not an option; it would have been tantamount to suicide.

Woldu took a deep breath. He couldn't believe it was all over. Not like this? Not after everything they had endured? Surely they wouldn't be sent back to the Lowlands now? Not when they were so close to home. He refused to believe it. The soldier nearest to them, an AK-47 swinging from his neck, gruffly beckoned the family forward.

'Where are you going?' he snarled at them, his hand reaching forward. 'I need your ID papers.'

'My ID card was burned when my house caught fire,' Woldu lied without hesitation.

The soldier got very angry and started screaming at him, his face just centimetres from Woldu's own. With spit flecking from his mouth, he yelled, 'Tell me the truth. You were resettled, weren't you? You are fugitives aren't you?'

Lemlem hid behind her mother's trembling legs. Birhan and Silas recoiled from the man, still sitting as they were on their father's shoulders. There was nothing Woldu could do. The Derg men led them away and held them captive beneath an old stone bridge over a trickle of mountain stream.

"I was terrified,' Woldu admits. 'The Derg men threatened to send us to a temporary camp nearby where they were holding people who were runaways. The soldiers knew all about the resettlement areas. They knew if they sent us back they were sending us to hell. It would have been heartbreaking but it would have been God's will.'

The girls didn't realize the danger that they were in and relaxing among the soldiers, began to play with one another and laughter filled the air. As the soldiers gulped down their coffee, Lemlem and Birhan, with the manners they had been taught, offered to wash their cups in the stream. The hours rolled by and they slept under the blankets beneath the bridge with the armed guards watching over them. The next day the adults were given coffee. The Derg officer finally said. 'Tell us the truth, now.' Woldu at last admitted that they were fugitives but said the reason that they had come back was that they had left a child behind in Tigray when they were resettled.

To Woldu's surprise, the soldiers told him that they could go. They told Woldu that anyone who could walk such a distance with his daughters on his shoulders shouldn't be arrested. They even showed him which route to take to avoid further Derg patrols. As a result the family avoided Maychew and took the safe route skirting the town which the gunmen had suggested.

Back in London that late June Bob Geldof was finalizing plans for his global Live Aid extravaganza. With the help of legendary concert promoter Harvey Goldsmith, he had persuaded a member of the world's most famous pop group The Beatles to appear on stage at London's Wembley stadium and similarly, for one of the Rolling Stones to appear live in Philadelphia. The supporting musical cast included The Who, David Bowie, Sir Elton John, Queen, a re-formed Led Zeppelin, Bob Dylan, Eric Clapton and, of course, the Queen of Pop at the time, Madonna. The heir to the British throne, Prince Charles and his glamorous young wife, Princess Diana, would be in the Royal Box at Wembley to witness it all.

Geldof had the world's attention. In the final two weeks before the US and UK shows were due to take place, Geldof set aside an hour and a half each day for interviews with the world media. During them, he would elaborate on the reasons for the concert and explain exactly why Africa desperately needed aid and development cash.

He had just finished an interview with the Canadian CBC TV team, led by reporter Terry Milewski, when the latter asked him to watch a short film the company had made. Speaking today from CBC's Toronto newsroom, Milewski, remembers the encounter well. He recalls that Geldof was 'strung out and trying to take a hundred calls'. He told the musician, 'Bob, you really have to take a look at it.'

'I really haven't time,' Geldof replied. 'I've another half dozen interviews to do before I can go.'

'Just watch the first minute. It's something one of our guys [Colin Dean] spliced together in the Hilton in Addis Ababa.'

Milewski pushed the tape into the machine and pressed 'Play'. A voice began to sing, *'Who's gonna tell you when it's too late...'* and the ghostly images of dying children from the hell on Earth of Mekele in the autumn of 1984 filled the screen. Geldof's eyes welled with tears. Towards the end of the shocking sequence Geldof stared intently at a little girl gulping in pain, seemingly breathing her last. It was the first time he had clapped eyes on Birhan Woldu. Terry recalls that Geldof went very quiet. He took the tape with him when he left but they had no idea what he was going to use it for. If it would be put to any use in Live Aid.

Geldof took the video to Goldsmith's office, which was a hive of frenetic activity. People instantly stopped what they were doing to watch it. Superstar David Bowie was there at the time. He broke down in tears as he watched and then offered to drop one of the songs from his set to accommodate it. Everyone watching it assumed that all the children featured in the film, Birhan included, had perished. It made them all the more determined to make the world aware of the scale of such a catastrophe.

Thousands of kilometres away on the bleak and windswept escarpment of the Ethiopian Highlands, an exhausted Birhan and the rest of the family traipsed on. The daily effort of carrying his daughters was now taking its toll on Woldu. His feet were blistered and bleeding and his lower back was in constant and piercing pain. One evening as the light failed a mother invited the family to stay in her mud-walled cottage. The next morning Woldu made the decision to jettison most of the family's meagre possessions. He was very weak now and wanted to save his strength for carrying the girls. He left a blanket, the ox skins, grain sacks and his sickle with her. Perhaps, he thought, he would be able to return one day to retrieve them. They set off again but Woldu was now struggling with chronic fatigue. They had been on the road for over two months now. All he could think was had he made the right decision? Should they have stayed in the resettlement area? Would they die before they reached Mekele?

Just as he was beginning to lose hope, he began to recognize the landscape, some of the villages they were passing through were places where he had traded cattle and goats. Within days they were on the outskirts of Kwiha, where Azmera had been buried after she perished in the Great Famine.

As they queued for food aid, they were amazed to find some of their neighbours from Lahama at the feeding camp. One old friend gave them five birr for bread, before saying: 'Leave at once. The Derg are resettling people from here all the time. It's not safe for you. Go to Lahama, there is a lot of fruit on the cacti there for you to eat.'

Before they set off they said their prayers outside St Mary's in Azmera's memory. Derg soldiers were crawling all over the countryside. One patrol even stopped them. They didn't realize the family were from the resettlement area and so they were allowed to pass.

It was an overcast afternoon when Woldu, Letebirhan and the girls finally descended into the familiar terraced fields of Lahama's winding valley. It was almost seven months since they had been forced onto the plane that had taken them to the resettlement area in the Lowlands. They were now greeted by the handful of villagers who had also returned to Lahama with the traditional Tigrayan welcome of bumping shoulders together. Woldu slumped down under the olive tree in the corral of his *sekela* hut. The wooden boughs of its roof had been taken by other villagers to use as firewood and its mud walls had begun to crumble.

At that moment it began to spit – it was raining 'God's Tears' (as the drops are known in Tigray). Birhan and Lemlem held their palms outstretched to the heavens and giggled as the droplets soon started washing the grime and dust of travel from their coffee-brown skin.

It had taken them two months and three weeks to get back from the resettlement area. They had travelled around 1,300km (800 miles), survived cholera, the Derg and so much more. Salty tears began to roll down Woldu's cheeks mixing with the raindrops. They had made it home. That day is seared into Woldu's heart. He insists he can even remember the actual date in the Ethiopian calendar. By following the saints days he knew that it was July 12, 1984 in the Western calendar. A day later, July 13, Live Aid would be broadcast.

It was the day that music changed the world.

AND THE
LESSON TODAY IS
HOW TO DIE...

London. July 13, 1984.

'IT'S 12 NOON in London; 7am in Philadelphia – and around the world it's time for Live Aid…', the voice boomed through Wembley Stadium's vast PA system.

Half a dozen trumpeters from the bearskin-clad Coldstream Guards played the first few bars of 'God Save the Queen', the British national anthem. Then, in a whirl of denim and long hair, Status Quo launched into 'Rockin' All Over The World'. The 72,000 delirious pop fans crammed inside the famous old North London stadium punched the air as one.

Gary Kemp, guitarist with Spandau Ballet, arrived at Wembley by helicopter. 'It hit us then, flying over the stadium and seeing the thousands of people coming in. There was this sense of a grand event going on that could equal England winning the World Cup in 1966 or the Coronation of 1953. This was something that would be stamped on everybody. It was a day when, no matter how young you were, you remembered where you were.'

The idea behind this monumental event, this Global Jukebox, was that it would be part-pop concert and part-telethon to raise the cash needed to help famine-struck Africans. Bob Geldof believed that it would also shame the international community to do more. During the Style Council's set he had slipped away from his place next to Prince Charles and Princess Diana in the Royal Box. He emerged on the giant stage to wild cheers with his group, The Boomtown Rats. It was almost impossible to recall that just the evening before Geldof had been terrified. His partner, Paula, had had to lay down white towels for him to sleep on because he was suffering from heavy cold sweats.

'I was shitting myself. If the bands didn't show up, 17 hours of The Boomtown Rats would have been a little too much for anybody,' he comments wryly.

'It was only when I walked on stage with the band that the romance of it and the hugeness of it got to me.'

The Rats broke into their international smash hit 'I Don't Like Mondays' to rapturous applause. Reaching the line in the song, *And the lesson today is how to die*', he paused with almost theatrical effect, punching his clenched fist in the air as the crowd hushed. He kept his fist aloft in the muted stadium for as long as he dared – an estimated two billion live television viewers in 60 countries around the world held their collective breath.

'Dare I say it, it was evangelical,' Gary Kemp comments.

In the United States, the Philadelphia show opened at 2pm local time with acclaimed folk singer Joan Baez announcing to the estimated 100,000-strong crowd that this was their Woodstock. Referencing the three-day iconic music festival that took place in 1969, she added 'and it's long overdue'. Baez led the crowd in a rendition of the hauntingly beautiful 'Amazing Grace' in an emotional scene that replicated the Wembley concert's outpouring of emotion.

A host of stars followed – Madonna bounded onto the John F. Kennedy stage in the blazing 35 degrees celsius heat, yelling 'I'm not taking shit off today!' in reference to the recent release of early nude photos of her in top-shelf magazines *Penthouse* and *Playboy*. English rock gods Led Zeppelin had re-formed and were joined onstage by Genesis singer and drummer Phil Collins who had played the Wembley leg before jetting across the Atlantic on Concorde. During their duet on 'It's Only Rock 'n' Roll', Mick Jagger ripped away part of Tina Turner's dress, leaving her to finish the song in what was, effectively, a leotard. During the day there were link-ups with other Live Aid events in Australia, Russia, Japan, Yugoslavia, Austria and Germany.

In London, nearly seven hours into the concert, Geldof was disappointed that only £1.2 million had been raised. He marched to the BBC commentary position where he was to be interviewed by presenter David Hepworth. The commentator was attempting to provide a list of addresses to which potential donations should be sent, but Geldof interrupted him in mid-flow, shouting, '*Fuck the address, let's get the numbers!*' It has passed into urban myth that he yelled at the audience, '*Give us your fucking money!*', but that phrase was never uttered. After the four-letter outburst, donations increased to £300 per second.

On stage, the Global Jukebox had reached a climax. David Bowie dedicated his soaring anthem 'Heroes' to his son, and to 'all our children, and the children of the world'. Bowie paused before introducing the CBC video that Colin Dean had spliced together, 'The subject speaks for itself. Please send your money in,' he said simply.

Audiences heard the melancholy keyboard refrain of The Cars' 'Drive' as Philippe Billard's extraordinary pictures filled the giant screens. There was the little boy, a crouching skeleton, too weak to stand. Then a piece of brown sacking wrapped with twine around the withered but unmistakeable outline of a child's skull and tiny body. And, in the final few frames, there was the gaping mouth and rolling eyes of a little girl, apparently slipping towards death. The camera rested on Birhan for a few moments.

The Wembley audience, until then euphorically beaming and dancing to the music played by the cream of 20th-century pop, were struck dumb. They weren't expecting this parade of suffering children, seemingly from another world. The response for many in the stadium and at home was tears. For others though it was action. The telethon pledge telephone system broke down completely, Geldof recalls, with people wanting to stop the atrocities they were witnessing on their screens. The video, also screened in the States and across the globe, stopped Live Aid in its tracks.

Terry Milewski was reporting inside the heaving stadium for CBC when he saw the images on the big screen. He had had no idea that Geldof was going to run the tape. 'It had been a real festive atmosphere until then, marijuana being smoked in the crowd – a real party. And then the place went quiet. People couldn't look away from the film. It captured the eye, as well as the heart. Everyone suddenly realized the reason we were all there.'

Colin Dean was listening to the radio as he drove through green fields towards an English coastal ferry port for a holiday in France when he heard The Cars' song begin. The man who made the inspiring film while crouched over an editing machine in an Addis Ababa hotel room didn't need to see the pictures. Every frame was hard-wired into his brain. The original tape is still sitting on the bookcase in Dean's French home.

When 'Drive' comes on the radio today he has to switch it off. The memories the song evokes are still too painful to bear. 'I just put it together,' he remarks. '[But] without Philippe's brilliant camera work, it wouldn't have happened.'

Red Cross nurse Claire Bertschinger was sitting on her settee at home in Britain watching the emotion-charged scenes, while feeling numb. She had returned only the previous month from Tigray after a year in the famine zone helping the helpless. It had taken a grim toll on her both mentally and physically. Now she was finding it difficult to equate the pop stars on TV belting out their hits with the suffering that she had personally witnessed around Mekele. She watched the video featuring Birhan and the other children with tears pouring down her cheeks, but she felt completely detached from all the emotion emanating from the crowd at Live Aid, all in the name of Ethiopia. She was later told that she was suffering from post-traumatic stress disorder (PTSD).

In Canada, watching the same images in his father's sunny Toronto garden, Brian Stewart also had no idea that Colin Dean's tape would be screened around the globe that day. The CBC correspondent was on leave, 'trying to relax and ease my mind' after the trauma of reporting for weeks on end from the famine epicentre in Tigray. The London-based reporter would later have regrets about not staying there for Live Aid but he had needed to go home.

Stewart admits: 'My nerves were quite shaky by this time, and I was thoroughly exhausted, emotionally and physically. I would not say I had post-traumatic stress disorder but certainly something close to it.'

He had planned to watch just the start of the concert but like millions around the globe found himself unable to switch the TV off. Unlike most of those millions watching Dean's video, he knew every shot, every starving child. He had witnessed it all first hand. He felt a special jolt in seeing Birhan again. He found the small child trying to stand on unsteady legs in the awful cold of that morning unbearably moving as well. He remembered how cold the dawns could be up in northern Ethiopia. Recalled just how exhausted everyone was. How very far from any feeling of hope, and how close to despair he and his CBC team were during those awful days. The explosion of world concern, the songs, videos, and now Live Aid would have been utterly unimaginable to Stewart and his team in November and December 1984.

'We had no idea then of the power of story, or of the revolution in worldwide volunteer work that it was to set off. My reaction, as the show ran on, was a mix of enormous hope for the immediate future, and real sadness for the recent past. Bob Geldof grasped, in a moment of real genius, what the rest of us did not – that the world not only would respond massively, but in ways that could transform the very way societies responded to humanitarian challenges like this.'

As he watched, Stewart was left wondering what had happened to the little girl who had miraculously come back from the dead. He knew all too well the precariousness of life in the war-ravaged Highlands. Could she possibly still be alive? He wondered if she could possibly have survived the famine, the civil war and the Derg's brutal resettlements?.

At Wembley, the bands played on. U2 singer Bono plucked a young girl who was being squashed from the crowd during a barnstorming performance that would turn the band into global superstars. Queen's Freddie Mercury led the 72,000 gathered there through a mass singalong to 'Radio Ga Ga'. Then the whole ensemble came back on stage for a mass rendition of 'Do They Know It's Christmas?', ending with conquering hero Geldof hoisted on the shoulders of former Beatle Paul McCartney and The Who's Pete Townshend. In Philadelphia, the concert similarly finished with a rousing group rendition of the song 'We Are The World'.

It is estimated that 85 percent of the world's TV sets were tuned into Live Aid that day. It was the biggest shared event in human history. In the spirit of music and charity, Geldof had unified the world, gained huge political leverage for banishing poverty and raised £150 million for famine relief in the process. Colin Dean's video had helped provoke the greatest surge in humanitarian giving in history. Birhan's face had literally stopped the world in its tracks. People in every continent gave not just materially but also something of themselves too.

'Cynicism and greed and selfishness had been eliminated for a moment,' Geldof later wrote. 'It felt good. A lot of people had rediscovered something in themselves.'

In dusty Lahama's scatter of thatched-roofed *sekela* huts in Ethiopia's remote north, Birhan's family knew nothing of this global coming together in that summer of 1985. Without access to TV or radio, the names of The Beatles let alone Bob Geldof meant nothing to them. They had no idea that Birhan's face was known to billions – billions who believed, for the most part, that she was now dead. Their epic 11-week journey from the Lowlands was a thunderous confirmation of the tenacity of the human spirit. Woldu believed it was 'God's power' that had led them back to their native soil. 'I thanked the Lord on my knees. The rains had come, the valley was green again and the neighbours had planted corn. They welcomed us back and gave us flour and bread.' Birhan remembers one family especially making a fuss of them. They kept kissing the girls, tearfully, saying, 'Poor Lemlem; poor Birhan'. Years later she discovered that they were her birth mother Alemetsehay's relatives – her own uncles, aunts and cousins.

Although they were now home, they had lost everything. They had no possessions, not even ox skins to sleep on, bedding down instead on the cold, bare earth, while their friends helped them make their tumbledown hut habitable again. Their neighbours gave them *injera* bread and they ate the ripening fruits of the abundant prickly pear cacti.

Woldu was overjoyed to have made it home with his three daughters and wife alive. However, the gargantuan effort had taken its toll on his health and had left him dangerously weak. A neighbour of Woldu's brought him ox skins to sleep on, but within a very short time he had developed a hacking cough and a raging fever and was suffering from sweats. As he lay in the hut, Woldu could hear the big summer rains deluging the newly woven straw of the hut's roof. The harvest would be good, but he was afraid that he wouldn't live to see it. 'I believed I would never see my grandchildren.'

The family became increasingly worried about Woldu and so the village elders decided to perform traditional medicine on him. 'They put a knife into my back, then sucked the bad blood out. After some time it made me better.'

When he was able to, Woldu began to work his little patch of land again. He had lost all his livestock in the famine. He didn't even have a plough ox to till the soil and so he worked by hand. He began weaving cotton on a ramshackle loom to sell to a local farmer; this made five birr a day. He also collected firewood to sell in Kwiha market. He was nothing if not tenacious and even his recent serious illness could not stop him from work. He was determined that his girls would never starve again.

Soon he had saved enough money to buy four goats. He then concentrated on building up his beehives again and with perserverance Woldu was soon the proud owner of 10. This meant he had enough surplus rich Tigrayan honey to sell in Kwiha or to exchange for bread. It took him a further three long years to save enough to buy a plough ox, but in that as in other things he was successful.

As he regained his strength Woldu also realized that he wanted another child and Letebirhan soon became pregnant. As with his first children, there were no problems. It seemed that God had doubly answered his prayers – the baby was a boy. He loved his girls but he would now have an extra pair of hands to help him with the plough oxen. Letebirhan was also overjoyed, but her baby was small and almost too weak to cry. Her happiness turned to anguish as the child failed to gain strength. Within nine days, the baby was dead. He hadn't even lived long enough to be given a name. The quiet sobs of grieving again filled the family *sekela*.

It seemed that life had slipped back to the rural grind that it had been before the Great Famine. Mornings began at first light when Lemlem and Birhan would slip their cotton smocks on and join the other barefoot children on the dusty track outside the collection of *sekelas*. They would traipse down to the river to get water, armed with an array of plastic bottles, old oil containers and clay pots. It was sometimes a trickle of water, sometimes a torrent, depending on the season. They would sing in unison most of the way there and back. Letebirhan would then prepare a breakfast of roasted wheat with milk from the cow, goat or sheep.

At the age of five, Birhan was expected to help out by herding the goats far into the mountains with her nine-year-old sister, Lemlem. The days were long and the girls would return exhausted at 7pm every evening, to enjoy a meal of *injera*, before going to bed soon afterwards. The family would sleep under the same blankets, on some ox skins, curled up together in the tiny hut. 'It helped us keep warm in those freezing nights and gave us real love as a family,' Birhan recalls fondly. 'It was alright unless someone couldn't sleep or snored. Then none of us slept.'

It wasn't an easy job, nor a particularly safe one. One day when she was tending her herd among the mountain scrub and heathland, she saw what she thought was a large mottled dog come bounding down the hill. It wasn't until it opened its black snout, revealing razor-sharp canine teeth that she realized that it was a marauding hyena. Before she knew it the beast had grabbed a billy goat by the throat and dragged it away while Birhan screamed in terror. Foxes were also a constant menace, but the girls would scare them off by screaming, waving their *dula* sticks and throwing stones.

The girls would also have playtime though. In a shaded square of grass and baked soil under olive and acacia trees, Birhan enjoyed endless games with the other children. She liked to win and loved *brima*, a sort of hopscotch using a grid marked out with a stick in the dust. Then there was *tibo*, which involved collecting a good few pebbles, keeping one in your hand and laying the rest on the ground. After this the pebble in your hand would be thrown into the air, while you tried to pick up as many as you could from the ground before catching the one you had tossed. Birhan says that the open-air playground 'was nothing fancy. We played with what we found among the trees and grass. We didn't have much but we were very happy.'

An inquisitive and bright child, according to her parents, Birhan had little outlet for her intellect or curiosity. There was no school in Lahama. No one in the family could read or write. Woldu taught the girls their prayers and every feast day the local priest would make a tour of each family hut. Sometimes he would perform exorcisms to ward off demons or *budas*. The Church played an important part in village life. As previously mentioned Christianity is important in Ethiopia. Woldu taught the girls to follow the calendar by saints days and feast celebrations. They were also instructed to cover their head with scarf when entering the church. In January at Timkat (epiphany), the whole village would troop down to the banks of the Mai-Shashasta river. The priest ducked every one of them in the clear mountain water to re-enact baptism. It was a time to renew vows and pray for the future.

Lahama and the surrounding area was still a battleground in the ongoing civil war between the Derg and the TPLF rebels. Sometimes the valley would echo with the sound of automatic gunfire. The families would then hide among the boulders strewn on the hillside until the fighting stopped. Woldu remembers the whistle of shells fizzing overhead as Derg artillery or tanks bombarded nearby TPLF positions from the direction of Kwiha. The rebels would sneak from their positions in the inaccessible mountains to beg for food from the villagers. They never used force and Woldu would send them away with *injera*. The Derg troops would demand goats, cattle and money while they waved their guns around.

The fighting often meant that it was too dangerous for Woldu to travel to the market to sell his precious honey and goats. Soon, food was again in short supply. In 1987, two years after Live Aid, a party of aid workers found their way to remote Lahama. They set about weighing and measuring all the children to see if any were malnourished. Birhan, now six, was judged healthy, but the baby of the family, four-year-old Silas was pronounced alarmingly underweight. The family was given food aid – ground wheat, pulses, powdered milk, biscuits and vegetable oil. It seemed as if their prayers had been answered once more and the family all grew strong again. In that same year, Letebirhan also became pregnant again and this time the baby, a girl named Medhine, survived. Woldu said that the new child just strengthened his love for Letebirhan.

Out on the wild alpine meadows, where the village children grazed their herds of goats and sheep, little Birhan now had more to contend with than just snarling foxes and hyenas. A gang of four village boys was bullying the girls and the smaller children. When Lemlem and Birhan took their livestock to the pastures the boys would tell them where their goats could or could not graze. The gang would laugh and throw stones at the girls as they herded their goats. 'They were very nasty,' Birhan recalls with displeasure. 'I remember they tied a smaller boy to a tree then made him shit and eat it. They acted like princes and would make us girls do all the work, forcing us to run after their stray goats. But I refused to let them bully me. I stood up to them.' Birhan would later pay for her courage.

When she was about seven, one of the bullies decided to punish her. She was tricked into following the boys into a strange area of moorland escarpment. It was high in the mountains and the few clumps of juniper trees were shrunken and bent by the strong winds. The boys then ran away and left her as it became dark. She was lost, alone and very scared. Birhan began to cry and shout for her father. Woldu, after much searching, eventually found her. She was three hours away from the village and had spent several terrifying hours on a lonely mountainside in the howling wind. The next time the boys teased them, the girls stood up to them. When the boys kicked Lemlem, Birhan screamed at her sister, 'Hit them back.' Then she charged the boys with fists and her *dula* flailing. As Lemlem joined in too, they beat the lads back. Birhan said that after that particular battle the boys left them alone. Woldu comments: 'That was Birhan. She would fight the boys even though she was the smallest. She was tiny but had such strong resolve. She stood up for her big sister who was four years older than her but didn't have the same confidence.'

And so life went on, until one windy day in 1988 when a stranger came into the village and asked to see Woldu. He told Birhan's father that he had to come to Kwiha at once, the government authorities needed to speak to him on an urgent matter. It was worrying news for the farmer, just as things were starting to look up for the family. What could the Derg possibly want with him now? Had they finally discovered that his family had escaped from the resettlement camp in the Lowlands? Would they make them return?

Woldu felt he had no choice other than to accompany the man across the mountains to Kwiha. This was his worst nightmare. Kwiha was where the family had spent the most difficult days of the Great Famine and where Azmera had died. When they arrived, Woldu was taken to a dilapidated government office in the tumbledown little town. He was told to sit down on a small wood and calfskin stool. A group of Derg officials crowded around him. He was terrified. Finally, one of the men pulled out a photograph. He stared at Woldu closely, then examined the picture. The man then barked at the others, 'It's him.' At that point, Woldu believed that he was done for. Then the official stuck the photo in Woldu's face, demanding, 'Where is she? What happened to your daughter?'

Confused by the turn of events, Woldu looked down at the photograph properly. He recognized the scene. How could he not? It was the clinic at Latchi. And there he was with little Birhan. It was the time of the Great Famine, when she had come back from the dead. He said a silent prayer. To the men around him, he explained that Birhan was very well and back at his *sekela* in Lahama from where he and his Derg companion had come.

'Why do you want us? What have we done?' he asked them. No one replied to his questions, instead he was just ordered to return to the village and come back to Kwiha, this time with his little daughter. There would be presents for her, new clothes, he was told, but he must leave at once.

Woldu thought the request very strange, but he did what he was told. These were the Derg after all and he had witnessed first hand just what they were capable of. After an exhausting journey back to Lahama, where he was unable to answer his family's questions, he returned one day later with his bemused seven-year-old daughter in tow. Birhan had asked him what was happening, but he had been unable to tell her and he didn't want her to worry. When they arrived at the offices, they were told to wait. The presents would come soon, they were assured, but they had to wait. Woldu and Birhan sat there, but the hours passed and night fell. They had no money, and Woldu was forced to beg for food before he cuddled up with his daughter under a blanket to sleep under the stars. The next day, they waited but nothing happened, and the next and the next. As the days passed, Woldu became more anxious. What was going to happen to them? He was perplexed. Surely if they were going to die or be resettled it would have happened by now?

After a week, they were sent for. This time they were packed into an old car. With growing trepidation, Woldu stared out of the window, watching Kwiha disappear into the distance. Would this be another long trip? His question was answered when the car stopped just minutes away at the crossroads town of Ashegoda. They were told to get out. As the car door swung open Woldu saw sacks and sacks of grain. There were also *farenjis* with cameras, too.

Birhan was startled. 'The only pale-skinned people I could remember were the angels I had seen painted on the walls of our churches.'

She stared at one of the group of men in front of her. He was looking at her particularly intently. Although she didn't recognize him they had met before. Brian Stewart had returned.

LIFE
AFTER DEATH

THE HORRIFIC slideshow crowded Brian Stewart's traumatized mind in his waking hours and in the quiet of the dead of night. He had been witness, after all, to the horrors of Mekele and Korem. It was 1988 and Live Aid was three years distant, a thing of the past for many of those who had watched Dean's video when it was beamed into their homes that day. For Stewart it was a different matter: the contorted faces of the starving, of people whose bodies were digesting themselves, of corpses littering the streets, just wouldn't go away. The cackle of scavenging hyenas as they gorged on human flesh – the living and the dead – still haunted him. 'I remember seeing the body of a woman half-devoured by hyenas. We raced her still living son to a clinic – he had half a hand bitten off. That kind of scene is hard to shake.'

Stewart, along with the BBC's Michael Buerk, had been the eyes and ears of a horrified world in Tigray in October 1984. Yet the 'biblical' scale of the hunger left the former with feelings of inadequacy. In 1988 he would write vividly of the after-effects on the psyche of those who had observed so much human suffering in Ethiopia's desolate mountains.

'We were able to postpone the final reckoning until our work was done. But later it hit with the force of a tidal wave, stunning us all as we stayed in a luxury hotel in Addis Ababa, or dined out later in London, or tried to sleep between clean sheets at home. For months afterwards I had nightmares. Night images of starving children and corpses piled in the green tent (the temporary morgue at Mekele). For a while I even learned once again to sleep with a light on to ease the shock when I awoke bathed in sweat.'

Stewart has interviewed many of the leading men and women of the time – Nelson Mandela, Margaret Thatcher, Polish Solidarity trade union founder Lech Walesa and US Secretary of State Henry Kissinger, among them, but it was Ethiopia's dark days of 1984 that would leave the most lasting impression. He believes that he will never really get over it.

'Initially there were few TV crews on the ground, and for a week or so, after the BBC ran into access problems, we seemed the only ones up near Korem and Mekele. The camp at Korem was losing 100 people a day, mostly children. Everywhere we went were lines of sick, starving and even the dead… I was also emotionally shaken by a sense of overwhelming sadness that such a proud, admirable and utterly blameless population would have to suffer so much. It seemed most of their history was a long record of suffering and at the time one wondered if there would ever be any way out.'

After Tigray everything seemed like a 'sideshow' to him. He kept thinking back to the scenes of human devastation and thinking, 'What the hell do I do about this myself?' Now based in Frankfurt, Germany, as the NBC's correspondent there, he was tiring of the conveyor belt of news reporting, of only covering disasters when he felt he could do so much more. He left NBC and considered joining an NGO to work in Africa. However, when he returned to Canada in 1987 CBC's highly regarded documentary unit *The Journal* approached him to do a series of specials, which would allow him to cover global issues in much greater depth.

Stewart's thoughts had often returned again and again to Birhan and Woldu. He wondered what had happened to the father and his frail child, the girl whose image, broadcast at Live Aid, now personified the suffering of her people for so many. Now, he had the opportunity to return to Ethiopia to put together a documentary on the country's recovery from the Great Famine – and the chance to track down Birhan. To at least discover if she was alive or dead. He didn't believe that the girl who had made the world sit up and listen at Live Aid should be forgotten as a footnote in history.

Along with producer Tony Burman, the man who had smuggled CBC's original 1984 famine reports out of Ethiopia taped to his back, Stewart began to plan how to get back into war-blighted Tigray. They would have to put themselves in the hands of an increasingly paranoid and embattled Derg, who were then struggling to control Mekele and Kwiha against a TPLF onslaught, and also seek help from locally based NGOs.

In early 1988, the two men flew back to Addis with more hope than confidence of ever finding Birhan. A search of feeding centres, resettlement camps and remote villages could take months, years perhaps, and even then might ultimately be unsuccessful. The Canadian Embassy in Addis had strongly impressed upon the Ethiopian government the need to let the CBC see how recovery efforts were progressing in the north. Still it seemed a daunting task, but then word came of a breakthrough. Little Silas's aid allowance was listed in official ration ledgers and alongside her entry were the names of Woldu and Birhan.

The CBC team caught the plane to Mekele. With Derg minders in tow, they drove to Ashegoda, some 17km (10 miles) from the Tigrayan capital, all the while their nerves jangling. Could it really be so easy? Could the Birhan listed be the girl they had filmed in 1984? Stewart was as suspicious of the Derg government as it was of him. The regime was well aware of the ramifications and importance of mass media coverage after the TV reports of 1984, which had focused the world's attention on Ethiopia, and Stewart and his team were equally aware that they were possibly being manipulated.

The CBC team pulled up at a roadside hamlet and the door of the van they were travelling in was pulled open. They climbed down. A car drew up across from them and a man, accompanied by a little girl, climbed out.

'My God! It's her,' Burman excitedly cried out.

Years of pent-up emotion rushed through Stewart. First of all an aching relief that this courageous father and his beautiful daughter were actually still alive, followed by an overriding joy that this was all real. But they had little time for pleasantries; Stewart and his team were conscious of the ever-watching Derg and were soon at work with camera and notepad in hand.

Birhan says that she was at first afraid of the white-skinned strangers, who stared at her so intently. She had been too young and sick to remember Stewart and his team. With no access to radio or TV, she had no concept of what the cameras were for or why they were so interested in her. Her only thought was: 'If anyone touches me, I'm going to run away.

Even Woldu only dimly remembered the *farenji*s from Latchi. At that time he had been more concerned with his dying daughter. Now, he had other worries: He still didn't know exactly what the Derg wanted or why they had brought them to the village. He was concentrating on not antagonizing the government officials, still aware that as far as they were concerned he and Birhan might just be runaways from the resettlement camps.

As he watched, their Derg minders explained to the *farenjis* that Woldu and Birhan's home was here in the village of Ashegoda. Woldu was instructed what to do. He showed the CBC team where he 'lived' in a little stone house with an old woman who was his 'sister'. Woldu carried a 50kg (110lb) sack of grain into his 'home' and gave it to his 'sister'.

'It was all lies,' he now insists. 'I had to go along with what the Derg told me to say. I was worried we would be tortured or shot if we didn't.' Today Stewart also says: 'I have no doubt the Derg lied to us, as they did at every step.'

The CBC team were shown the food aid and watched as sacks of wheat were unloaded. The village women ululated (a long, wavering, high-pitched trilling) with pure joy. Birhan was awestruck. She had never seen such a crowd before. 'The authorities told them this food had come because of me. So many people were kissing me,' she recalls.

The real truth was that Woldu and Birhan's home Lahama was too dangerous for Derg officials and Western journalists. The inaccessible mountains around the river valley were crawling with TPLF rebels and that was not the message that the Derg junta wanted CBC to show the world. But time was short and the Derg was eager to move the CBC journalists on. While Tony Burman distracted their minders, Stewart was able to stuff a sheaf of birr notes into Woldu's tunic. Then, far too soon for Stewart's liking, they were parted again. This time he promised himself that he wouldn't lose touch with Woldu and Birhan, not now that he had found them in such difficult cirmcumstances.

155

Although Woldu had to leave behind the 50kg (110lb) of wheat that he had carried to his 'sister', he was just happy that the Derg had not detained them further. He returned home and with the money that the *farenji* had given him, he was able to buy bread. Birhan went back to goat herding and playing with her friends and sisters, only occasionally sparing a thought for the odd pale-skinned men she and her father had met.

When Stewart's documentary 'Life After Death' was screened in Canada in March 1988, it was met with widespread acclaim. It further pressurized the government to do more to support Ethiopia. Although Birhan's story resonated with Stewart, he hadn't been fully prepared for how it would connect with the people back home. The fact that she had survived against the odds meant that Birhan had become a symbol of hope not just for her own troubled homeland but also for all the world's children who led lives blighted by gross poverty, conflict and catastrophe.

Stewart wanted to help the family but knew he would have to act extremely carefully. He was aware that the Derg might not look favourably on a relationship between a member of the international press and the family. He was also worried about what effect shining the spotlight of publicity might have on the lives of these unassuming farming people. 'My sense was she had a wonderful father and their emotional closeness was very touching,' he now says. 'My idea was that with some help Birhan's family might find a better, more permanent residence and, most importantly, she could get an education and grow up to have a good and happy life in a new Ethiopia.'

Back in Mekele, Stewart met up with the large, bearded, and energetic Salesian monk Brother Cesare Bullo, who ran the Catholic Church's Dom Bosco Technical Training Centre. Brother Bullo had been a leading figure in organizing local NGOs in Mekele during the 1984 famine and in demanding outside relief. In the brief moments that the Derg minders allowed Stewart, he told the father that he wanted to pay to get Birhan, at least, established in a local primary school.

When Brother Bosco subsequently established contact with the family, Woldu said that he would be delighted for his daughter to receive an education, one that might allow her a brighter future. Lahama, however, had no school.

After careful consideration, Woldu decided that they would have to move to Kwiha, even though it had so many painful associations for the family. Woldu is not someone who dwells on bad memories. 'That was the past,' he says. 'All I could see was light. It was a light towards the future – a new bright future for the children. After everything we had been through it was wonderful. I felt I could now die happy. God had listened to our prayers.'

With the money Stewart had donated, a little stone cottage with a corrugated zinc roof resting on eucalyptus boughs was built on a site close to the feeding centre that had helped Birhan in 1984. It was much more spacious and comfortable than their *sekela* and had a little yard for chickens and a milking cow. They were able to move into the new home in September 1989, but Lemlem stayed behind in Lahama. Although only 13 she was married to a local teenager. By 15 she would have a child of her own. In remote villages, Woldu explains, it was then common for girls to be betrothed, if not actually married, at as young an age as 10. That might have been Birhan's lot, but for Brian Stewart. 'I didn't want to be married at 13 like Lemlem. Brian saved me, he's like a second father to me.'

After the move, Woldu continued to walk over the mountains to farm his land in Lahama. Birhan was excited by the move and a chance of another life other than the drudgery of the fields. She would now have a bed to sleep on for the first time, which she shared with Silas. They would talk long into the night about their exciting new world. Later they were astonished to watch television for the first time when a neighbour bought a set.

'I thought it was magic,' Birhan revealed. 'I couldn't understand how the people could fit inside it.'

Her new life meant adapting quickly to other aspects of the modern world. In 1990 when nine-year-old Birhan enrolled at Kwiha Elementary School for her first ever lessons, she had to catch up with her peers. Some of the other children in the 75-pupil class had already been taught some reading and writing by their parents. Also, with their traditional smocks and plaited hair, Birhan and her sister Silas were teased by the Kwiha boys for being country bumpkins.

'Our clothes and hair set us apart,' an unsmiling Birhan says. 'They called us "country girls", which was a big insult. The boys teased us and punched us, but gradually we started to dress in a more modern way in Western clothes. We still kept our traditional clothes for feast days and family occasions. Our culture is very important to us.'

As Birhan's primary school years progressed, Kwiha and Mekele both became key battlegrounds as the civil war reached its bitter denouement. She remembers a strafe attack by a Derg helicopter; it was like a giant vulture swooping down on the town. The terrified family ran for their lives, hiding amid a rocky outcrop on a nearby hill. They prayed each day at St Mary's for peace and for the TPLF to rid them of the Derg.

In June, 1988, the rebels took Mekele and a united force of Tigrayan and Eritrean fighters were on the road to Addis. One of Africa's most bloodthirsty regimes was finally crumbling. On May 21, 1991 the 'Black Stalin' Colonel Mengistu chose not to make a final stand and instead fled by jet to Zimbabwe where he remains today under the protection of fellow despot Robert Mugabe. One week later the rebels were celebrating in the Ethiopian capital. It would later mean Eritrean independence.

Birhan was told the news by friends in Kwiha. She joined the women shrilly ululating jubilantly in the streets. A new Ethiopia had dawned. She could barely contain her excitement.

After church in the morning, Birhan would set off for her primary school. She would weave through the streets filled with donkeys laden with huge bundles of scavenged tree branches and moth-eaten horses pulling carts weighed down with building stone. Returning to the stone-walled school today Birhan is mobbed by dozens of youngsters in threadbare green pullovers, a uniform seemingly handed down from generation to generation. The flags of Tigray Province and Ethiopia flutter on sturdy poles above a dusty football pitch. Maps of the world and Ethiopia are painted on one wall, the human heart and a foetus in the womb on another.

Birhan was the fastest runner among the girls in her class. 'I must get the athletic ability from Woldu and all his walking,' she smiles. She speaks of being inspired by her maths teacher, Asefu Teshorme. 'One morning I was late, I overslept and decided to have a long breakfast at home. When I finally got to school Asefu said: "Go home and tell your parents to come and see me." When Ato Woldu arrived Asefu told him that education was a wonderful privilege and that I shouldn't be late like that. I made sure it didn't happen again.'

The teacher now works at another school nearby. A white shawl with brilliant green and gold trimming covering her jet-black hair, Asefu insists: 'Education is key to developing Ethiopia. We didn't have a chance of attending class before, especially the girls. I wanted to impress that on Birhan. After that she would always put in the effort. Her marks were average in class but she was always working hard and asking questions.'

Birhan moved on to the Woldu Negus secondary school in Kwiha in 1996, at the age of 14. She would stroll through the sandy, rock-strewn roads, her exercise books tucked under her arm, with best friends, Abadit and Firewoini. They would laugh and laugh as they talked about boys, Tigrinya music and dancing. She studied maths, English, biology, geography, Tigrinya, Amharic and the history of Ethiopia, including the reign of Haile Selassie and the tyranny of the Mengistu years. In the rainy season the family would go back to Lahama to sow, plough and spend time with Lemlem and her children. Here she saw the back-breaking relentless grind of her sister's life and the precariousness of bringing up children there. It brought home how lucky she was to be able to leave that life behind.

Now fairly prosperous, Letebirhan and Woldu had four more children, Tirhas, Haftu, Solomon and Senait. Birhan loved mothering the little ones, but she also worked hard to get the grades to pursue her dream of going to university to become a nurse. Childhood visits to Kwiha hospital with various family members and time spent observing the medics in their white, starched tunics convinced her of that. She also wanted to help look after her little brother, Haftu, who had limited use of his limbs following a bout of measles. She helped feed and clothe him and did some simple physiotherapy exercises to help get him to use his limbs. Her Orthodox religion was still central to her life. She adored church music, fasted at the right times and always said her prayers.

Everything seemed to be going well, but then the storm clouds of war descended upon Ethiopia once more. In May 1998 fighting erupted with neighbouring Eritrea over a disputed 390 square km (150 square mile) scrap of land on their shared border called the Yirga Triangle. One commentator said the conflict between the two desperately poor nations was like 'two bald men fighting over a comb'. The bitter fighting

160

Previous page: Birhan in the family compound in Kwiha in October 2004 during her first interview with The Sun. *(Arthur Edwards/*The Sun*)*

*Right: Birhan's father, Woldu. A lifelong farmer, he was born in c.1948 during the reign of Emperor Haile Selassie. (Arthur Edwards/*The Sun*)*

Above: Birhan's stepmother, Letebirhan. (Oliver Harvey)

Above: A teenage Birhan (left) in Kwiha with two school friends in about 1997.
(Birhan Woldu Collection)

Above: Birhan's family at home in Kwiha. Top row, from left to right: fiancé Birhanu, Birhan, father Wolda, stepmother Letebirhan, sister Silas and half-brother Hafta. Front row, from the left: niece Masho, half-brother Solomon, half-sister Tirhas and half-brother Senait. (Oliver Harvey)

Above: Birhan meets Bob Geldof (left) and Tony Blair (right) at the Commission for Africa summit in Addis Ababa in October, 2004. Blair clutches the Lalibela cross that Birhan had presented him with just moments earlier. (Arthur Edwards/The Sun)

Above: Birhan with Hollywood star Brad Pitt backstage at Live 8 in Hyde Park on July 2, 2005. Birhan had no idea who he was at the time. (Oliver Harvey)

Above: Bisrat Mesfin and Birhan with David and Victoria Beckham backstage at Live 8. Bisrat, a huge fan of English football, was delighted to meet the former Manchester United star. Birhan didn't recognize either of the Beckhams. (Oliver Harvey)

Above: Bisrat, Bob Geldof, Birhan and author Oliver Harvey at the opening of Hagere Selam School in Tigray in November, 2009. It was built with a £85,000 grant from Band Aid. (Oliver Harvey)

Above: Birhan and fiancé Birhanu celebrate their engagement in January, 2010.
(Birhan Woldu Collection)

reached Mekele in June of that year. Eritrean war planes screamed over the mountains dropping cluster bombs on civilian areas, including a primary school, leaving over 50 civilians dead and dozens wounded. Birhan heard the roar of the jet engines and cowered as they flashed passed. She was terrified that the bloodshed of the Derg years would return to blight her cherished Tigray.

In the end tens of thousands died on both sides as fighting erupted along the border until a peace accord was signed in December 2000. Tensions still simmer today and it is currently impossible to cross the border between the two countries.

Hearing the news of the Mekele air raid at home in Canada, Brian Stewart was terrified that it was Birhan's school that had been hit. Surely after all she had been through it wouldn't end like this? Although he had tried to maintain correspondence with the family, while allowing them space to lead a normal life, he had lost touch with them. When he heard that Mekele had fallen to the rebels back in 1988, he had various ideas of how to get there, even the 'nutty' idea of reaching Tigray by mule or horseback.

Distraction came when he was sent to report on the first Gulf War in 1991. On returning to Canada though he again began to wonder about Birhan. Toronto by then had an estimated 5,000-strong population of Tigrayan refugees and immigrants, many of whom ran the city's car parks. Every time he parked his car Stewart would ask any Ethiopians: 'Are you from Mekele?' Amazingly, he eventually found someone who not only knew Kwiha but Woldu's family as well. Through their contacts, he was able, several times a year to send CAN $100 or so, in cash inside a letter with a traveller returning to

Tigray. Although this was a precarious way of sending money and he had no idea of whether it was getting through or not, it paid off. By 1992, he was getting letters back. Birhan would write letters in her Tigrinya language, which Stewart would then have translated back in Canada.

'It was a weak system, and some years we almost fell out of touch altogether. I was never entirely sure all the modest amounts of money I sent went in the right direction,' he admits. Birhan remembers the letters well and was thankful for the contact with the man whom she had come to see as a saviour.

Ethiopia kept pulling Stewart back. In 1994, he led a CBC team there for a 10th-anniversary documentary of the Great Famine to show how the country was getting back on its feet. He was once more able to meet up with Birhan. Now he was able to put his financial help for the family on a more firm footing. Abba Hagos Woldegiorgis, head of the Catholic Secretariat in Mekele, helped Stewart set up bank accounts for Birhan and Woldu. After this he was able to send off regular annual payments to them. However, Woldu was very mistrustful of banks and said that he didn't want to use them as he was worried they might take the money Stewart deposited.

In 2002 Stewart was back in the Highlands again to report on Ethiopia's progress since the famine. For CBC's travel arrangements he used a travel company in Mekele run by a good-humoured and proficient manager called Bisrat Mesfin. After hearing about the CBC man's problems in transferring funds to Birhan, Bisrat said: 'Mr Stewart, perhaps I can help you?'

Dressed in sharp business suits and pressed white shirts, Bisrat has the appearance and demeanour of a successful multinational chief executive or even a charismatic politician. Many of those who meet him are confident that he could easily do both. Instead he has devoted much of his life to helping disadvantaged children in his native Tigray be empowered through education. For his inspiration, Bisrat draws on his own turbulent childhood and experiences. He was born in Mekele around 1979. His civil-servant father was often absent from home. His mother, who was a cook in a relief centre in Mekele, would bring back leftovers to feed her nine children. It was never enough and so they also relied on international aid to eat. Bisrat can remember going to school with the pockets of his shorts full of roasted wheat from aid sacks. 'It was my lunch. If someone had bread I would exchange it for the wheat.'

He slept on ox skins in their tiny, mud-walled home, huddled together with his elder brother, Goitom, to keep warm and dreamed of another life. 'I wanted to be a doctor or a pilot – that was bullshit, of course.'

Three months after the TPLF captured Mekele, Bisrat's father took him from the war-blighted and hungry town to neighbouring Eritrea, walking much of the way. They ended up staying in a refugee camp for a month, surviving on a couple of bread rolls a day. It was the worst time of his life. He later fled back to Ethiopia to see out the civil war with his sister, Alemetsehay, in Dessie, south of Mekele.

After the Derg fell in 1991, Bisrat returned to Mekele to a life of hawking cigarettes and chewing gum in the streets to pay for food and his exercise books. The family's shack was so close to the city's Green Hotel that he could smell their *injera* cooking. 'I was so thin. I went to the hotel and offered to do odd jobs for them. They would give me leftover *injera*. I met *farenjis* and began to learn English from them.'

In 1993 a stiff-backed, white-haired, pipe-smoking *farenji* arrived at the hotel. The 14-year-old Bisrat offered to help him with his bags. Sometimes the *farenjis* could be snappy with the street children hustling cigarettes, but this one was polite and kind. Bisrat acknowledges that meeting was the one that changed his life forever. The man's name was David Stables.

A former captain in the British Army, he now worked for the International Red Cross in Ethiopia; he was also hungry after a long drive. The precocious teenager informed him that there was no restaurant at the hotel but that he knew just the place where the man could eat. On the way Bisrat, in broken English, proved to be witty, charming and bursting with confidence. When Stables asked the boy why he was selling gum and cigarettes, Bisrat said it was so that he could eat, help feed his family and continue his own schooling. Stables liked the boy and knew that he couldn't abandon him to the vagaries of the street.

Yorkshire-born accountant's son Stables was brought up in the post-war world of food rationing, home-grown vegetables and hand-me-down clothes. His relationship with Africa dates back to the mid-1960s when, as a British Army officer, Captain Stables was seconded to train local forces in the newly independent Kenya. Soon he was helping to build roads and airfields along the Kenyan border with Ethiopia and Somalia. After studying development at Oxford's Ruskin College, he worked in 1992 as a team leader for CARE International in war-ravaged Somalia. Encountering the international media here for the first time, Stables wasn't impressed and described their behaviour as 'often appalling'. He was working for the Red Cross in Mekele when he met Bisrat and took him under his wing, helping the boy with his education. Bisrat says it was the first time that he received 'proper food and proper love'.

A number of other underfed children began gravitating to Stables's bungalow. Soon he was also helping them to stay in school; he gave them hearty meals and the cast-off clothes that he brought back with him from his trips to Britain.

When Stables left for Tanzania in 1997, he wanted to carry on supporting the children and so the African Children's Educational Trust (A-CET) was born – to channel funds from donors to help vulnerable Ethiopians through education. Today Stables runs A-CET from a cramped £26-a-week council flat in a suburb of Leicester in Britain's Midlands. When Birhan later asked Stables why he lived in such a cramped apartment he told her that it was because he wanted to help as many Ethiopian children as he could. By 2002, A-CET pupil Number One, its first graduate Bisrat Mesfin, had a diploma in business management, another in tourism and was also helping Stables administer the NGO. At Bisrat's suggestion, in 2003, the two men then launched the NGO Ethiopia Youth Educational Support (EYES), as the local implementing partner for A-CET's funds.

'I am very, very proud of my country' Bisrat says. 'When you look up "famine" in the *Oxford English Dictionary* it gives the example of Ethiopia. I wanted to change that and the best way of doing it is through education. David Stables had helped me and now I felt I had a responsibility to help my own people.'

They make a curious double act: the pipe-smoking septuagenarian ex-British Army officer and the snappy-dressing 30-something famine survivor. Yet, A-CET's results have been little short of phenomenal. Once shoeshine boys and cigarette hawkers, A-CET graduates include 29-year-old Sammy Assefa, who made the seemingly unlikely journey from the straw-roofed shacks of Tigray to the Sanger Institute in England, where he conducted PhD research into the DNA of malaria-carrying mosquitoes in an effort to combat the disease that kills 781,000 a year around the globe. It is an amazing reflection of what education has the potential to achieve in Ethiopia and across Africa.

For Stewart, meeting Bisrat was a 'godsend'. Finally he could stop fretting about getting his donations to Birhan's family and how they were surviving – and so in 2002 Birhan and her six brothers and sisters became A-CET students. 'Everyone went to school because of Brian Stewart,' Birhan says. 'He sent money every month. He was like the father to all of us.'

David Stables remembers meeting Birhan for the first time. She was initially excessively shy around him but 'beautiful, dignified and utterly trusting'. Her reticence around him disappeared as he became a friend and advisor. The A-CET Chief Executive found her father, Woldu, 'a man touched by God'. Stables remembers the elderly man telling him: 'We must have been bad, very bad, for God to punish us so. But He saved Birhan and I so that He must have something for us to do for Him.'

Birhan sat her exams later in 2002, confident of getting into university to study nursing. She was thus heartbroken when her grades, although average, weren't good enough for her to get to university. Now suddenly, her dream of helping others as she had been helped all those years ago by the nurses at Latchi was out of her reach. She felt guilty and believed that she had let everyone down. What could she do now?

She spent months mooching around the family home in Kwiha helping Letebirhan with the household chores and weaving *injera* baskets from multicoloured straw to hang as wall ornaments. She couldn't find a job and she felt hopeless. Had it all been a waste of time? Had Brian Stewart wasted all his time and money? She was miserable. From somewhere she found the strength to pull herself out of the mire she was in. She began to focus and after a year of listlessness, finally she applied for a place on the three-year plant science degree course at Wukro Agricultural College. To her utter delight she was accepted.

An 80-minute bus journey north from Kwiha, Wukro gave Birhan independence. She missed home, especially Ato Woldu, but she found the Wukro people extremely friendly and hospitable. The bustling town had a distinct smell caused by the Sheba Tannery. There were nearby ancient rock-hewn churches to explore and offer prayers in and college social life was exciting. Birhan found comfortable lodgings, renting a room in a family home of stone walls and a corrugated tin roof. She soon made new friends, including a beautiful girl her own age called Alamnesh. The pair soon became a fixture in the coffee shops, where students could sit on cow-skin stools arranged outside on the dusty pavements. They also liked the clothes markets of Wukro. Sometimes the girls would enjoy a glass of tart, local Axumite red wine or a refreshing bottle of Ethiopian St George beer. At other times they would dance to rhythmic Arabic-tinged traditional music, with their hands on hips, rolling their shoulders, their heads jerking upwards and outwards. It was a mesmerizing and joyous time.

No matter how much she enjoyed herself, she was always on time for her lessons. She had never forgotten her primary school teacher Asefu Teshorme's talk about the importance of an education. That it was a privilege that shouldn't be squandered. She also met a boy called Birhanu with whom she had much in common. He was a famine survivor, too. He had been badly burned as a boy; his cheek was scarred and the top of his ear was missing. They had much to talk about over rich *bune* coffee, served in the traditional manner in tiny porcelain cups, and over evening meals of *injera*. She considered him another brother.

Brian Stewart and A-CET helped fund Birhan through college. She was also careful with her finances, saving up from the pocket money her father gave her to buy a pair of white training shoes and later her first pair of blue jeans. Like Ethiopia itself, she was embracing the outside world. Yet she also cherished her traditional culture and upbringing. On feast days she would wear her hair braided on her scalp in the traditional Tigrayan manner and she would wear her best embroided *shamma* shawl, while observing the Orthodox fasting time.

Over time, Bisrat became a mentor to her. He told her all about Band Aid, Live Aid and Bob Geldof, showing her the videos that David Stables had amassed. She saw the pictures of herself famished, '15 minutes from death' and marvelled at the tears of the *farenji* strangers watching in Wembley Stadium. Birhan comments: 'I realized I had a responsibility to my country and the memory of those who had died. My father always said God had spared me for a reason.'

When the BBC's Michael Buerk returned in 2003 to make a 20th-anniversary documentary on the famine, he contacted Birhan and asked to interview her.

Claire Bertschinger, the Red Cross nurse, who had to choose who lived and died two decades before, also returned with Buerk to confront her demons. Birhan and Claire, two women from such vastly different backgrounds, hit it off, quickly establishing a close friendship.

After the film crew left, Birhan and Bisrat talked late into the night, reliving the trauma of their individual and shared pasts, and that of their nation, with one another. Both had benefitted from the help of strangers, men who had, through kindness and concern, changed the paths that they would follow, giving them both untold opportunities. Birhan realized that her father's words were true; she had been spared for a reason, one that she had yet to find out. Bisrat also recognized that he and Birhan had met for some purpose.

'We had a journey together,' he now says. And it was a journey that would lead them to places and people they could never possibly have imagined – a journey that would help change both their lives and those of others, forever.

AN INSPIRATION
TO MILLIONS

TONY BLAIR was experiencing one of the most fraught years of his premiership. It was 2004 and his second term as British Prime Minister was mired in the bloody disaster of the Iraq invasion. No weapons of mass destruction had been found – and that had been a key reason for Britain and its coalition partners going to war. The Labour leader's boyish looks had began to look more strained, his hair greyer. On October 1 he had been treated in hospital for an 'atrial flutter', an irregular heartbeat, but just six days later he was in Africa, a continent he had described at the Labour Party conference in 2001 as 'a scar on the conscience of the world'.

Blair was in Addis Ababa for a meeting of the Commission for Africa (CFA), which he had founded in 2003 at the behest of Bob Geldof. The Live Aid guru had been travelling in Ethiopia and had witnessed food shortages that were potentially more catastrophic than the Great Famine of 1984. He again saw the agonizing sight of hungry people queuing for food to keep themselves alive.

Geldof was consumed with the same burning rage he had experienced when he had seen Michael Buerk's BBC TV reports on the famine 19 years earlier. While still in Africa, Geldof telephoned Downing Street and demanded to be put through to the Prime Minister, who was attending the G8 summit of the world's eight most powerful nations in Evian, France.

'It's happening again.' Geldof exploded at Blair.

Blair established the CFA with Geldof becoming a commissioner. The British leader saw it as a vehicle to put Africa (along with climate change) at the top of the agenda for Britain's simultaneous presidencies of the G8 and the EU in 2005. The goals were African debt relief, more aid and fairer trade. In the grand, circular assembly hall of the UN building in Addis, the thrust of Blair's speech was that a more economically stable Africa would be to the West's advantage.

'We know that poverty and instability leads to weak states, which can become havens for terrorists and other criminals,' he explained. He asserted that most African countries were still as poor as they had been 40 years earlier and that because of the HIV/AIDS pandemic, life expectancy in some nations had declined to what it had been in the 1950s.

Afterwards Blair and Geldof were led by sharp-suited aides through the labyrinthine corridors of the vast, concrete UN building to an anteroom lined with creaky traditional wooden Ethiopian sofas. Suddenly a connecting door opened and there before them stood Birhan Woldu, the child who 'died' on the big screens at Live Aid. She smiled at them serenely, with all the proud grace and sureness of an Abyssinian princess. Her hair was styled in the Tigrayan manner. It appeared very dark against her white embroidered tunic and traditional gleaming white shawl arranged loosely around her shoulders.

Blair and Geldof were shocked into open-mouthed silence. After being beckoned forward, Birhan approached the dark suited Blair and elegantly shook hands with him, seemingly unfazed by meeting one of the world's most powerful men. She then moved towards Geldof, dressed in a pin-striped suit and black trainers. He looked intensely into her brown eyes as he greeted her. The Prime Minister sat down and stared at the beautiful Ethiopian woman before him.

This astonishing meeting had been engineered by my newspaper *The Sun*. I was at Birhan's side scribbling in my notebook as the paper's veteran photographer Arthur Edwards snapped away. I showed Blair the original picture of Birhan, which the CBC team had taken as she lay emaciated, just minutes from death. Birhan, via her friend and mentor Bisrat Mesfin who was translating, told the two men about her plant science studies at university and her dream of being a nurse.

Suddenly, away from the formal summit meetings and long-winded speeches, Blair was confronted with the reality of what aid and development could mean to Africa. To a human being. Of all the hope and possibility that can come from saving just one life. There were millions upon millions of Birhans across Africa.

Close to tears, the Prime Minister whispered: 'Birhan, do you realize your image has been an inspiration to millions?'

Yes, she replied. She knew and was 'very grateful'. A clearly moved Blair added: 'I remember watching Live Aid and seeing Birhan. It was an inspiration to me in politics.'

How had the 'lost child' come to be at this extraordinary meeting?

Just five days earlier, I had been seated on a white-liveried Ethiopian Airlines twin-propeller plane as it came in fast and low over Tigray's mountains. With me were Arthur Edwards and an old friend Anthony Mitchell, who was now the

Associated Press (AP) newswire's 'Man in Addis'. From the little porthole window we could see clumps of thatched-roofed *sekela* huts dotting the cactus-strewn landscape like clusters of button mushrooms, many reached by dirt roads or winding rocky paths that were little more than goat tracks.

We were expecting a long and bumpy drive in a 4x4 through the bleak mountains to some remote village in the back of beyond that windy and sun-drenched October morning. It could take days. Collecting our bags from the carousel, we strolled through Mekele airport's cavernous, modern and near-empty glass-fronted arrivals hall. There in the mid-distance was a beautiful Tigrayan woman holding aloft a large piece of white cardboard. The words scrawled on the card in black marker pen soon came into focus. '*Mr Oliver*'. To our complete surprise it was unmistakeably the miracle girl of Live Aid, more beautiful in the flesh that any photograph could possibly portray.

In a brown zip-up cardigan and ankle-length brown-and-white skirt, the young woman facing us smiled and shook hands with us warmly, welcoming us to Tigray. In my shoulder bag I had a still photograph of Birhan taken just a short drive away at Latchi in 1984, her eyes rolling horribly back into her head as she apparently breathed her last. The delicate features may have been recognizable, but Birhan's brown eyes were now ablaze with life.

It was October 3, 2004 – some three weeks shy of the 20th anniversary of Michael Buerk's landmark reports and we were in Tigray to put together a series of features for *The Sun*. The previous year I had read about Birhan after she had been interviewed by Buerk for a BBC documentary and had found out that she was being supported by a charity called A-CET.

After making some enquiries, I called founder David Stables at his two-roomed Leicester council flat. Stables was blunt and to the point. In his long experience as an aid worker he had found many of the international media to be self-serving and arrogant. Following a long conversation, during which I made many assurances to Stables, he agreed to give me the telephone number of Bisrat, his man on the ground in Mekele. In the end, it was Anthony, who called Bisrat to arrange transport and hotels and within a day of leaving London we found ourselves in Tigray's mountains.

Birhan suggested we drive to her family's home in nearby Kwiha for our interview. Smiling Bisrat was on hand to translate. As we now skirted the airfield in Bisrat's white 4x4 he pointed out the landing strip where the Hercules aid flights had landed during the 1984 famine and also where the Antonov resettlement planes, carrying people like Birhan and her family, had flown out.

Soon we were at the gates of the family's tin-roofed cottage and were greeted by Woldu, dressed in his best but somewhat frayed pale suit and plastic sandals. We shook hands and bumped our right shoulders together in the traditional Tigrayan way. A more humble and dignified man it would be difficult to meet.

Passing through a yellow-painted solid iron gate, we entered a dusty yard shaded by an olive tree. A brown bantam hen with gleaming black tail feathers and her clutch of fluffy yellow chicks pecked in the brown dust in the yard. A dun-coloured cow, a large hump on its neck, stood tethered and munching on hay. Letebirhan was busy as ever in the kitchen baking barley in a sort of large metal wok over a fire of burning cow dung. Now we met Birhan's half-brother, Solomon, and half-sister, Medhine, who politely shook hands with us.

We found ourselves soon settled in armchairs, the best seats in their comfortable stone-walled house. It took a few seconds for our eyes to adjust after walking from the intense sunshine of midday into the darkened room. Multicoloured woven straw *injera* storage baskets lined the walls. In one corner was a wooden bed covered with woollen blankets where 23-year-old Birhan slept next to her younger sister Silas. On the other side of the room sat a small chest of drawers bearing some Chinese-made plastic flowers, a wooden model of the monumental *stelae* standing stones from the ancient Ethiopian city of Aksum, found to the north of Mekele, and also a large, framed photograph of a dark-haired, middle-aged Western man. Birhan explained that his name was Brian Stewart and that he was like a 'father' to her.

Perched on a calfskin stool, Birhan began to perform Ethiopia's famous coffee ceremony. Coffee, named after Ethiopia's former Kaffa Province in the south-west, is a gift this nation gave to the world and is still vital to its export economy today. She roasted the beans on a little saucepan over glowing coals, wafting the aromatic fumes to each guest individually. Pungent incense burning in a little brazier made from an old USAID oil can was also fanned through the gloom. She then ground the beans in a wooden mortar and pestle and placed the coffee in a brown pottery boiling pot with a spherical base and a long neck.

Bringing the coffee to the boil, she poured it through a filter made from horsehair. Birhan then served the rich, dark brew in tiny, handleless white ceramic cups. We were encouraged to take three tea spoons of sugar, which added to the heady caffeine rush.

Although Birhan spoke some English she preferred to speak through her friend Bisrat translating. Bisrat explained that it is a great honour to take part in the ceremony and that it is considered impolite to leave before drinking a third cup, the *baraka* or 'blessing' cup.

The interview that took place with Birhan and her father Woldu both talking was, at times, overwhelming with sadness and, at others, gloriously uplifting. Birhan was friendly and welcoming but a little shy around *farenjis*. She said that she had often wondered why of all the thousands of dead and dying children on that godforsaken plateau around Mekele that it was her that the CBC cameras had picked out. She spoke movingly of how her family had been forced to accept emergency food provided by Western donors like Band Aid. Now she wanted a job where she could help the children of her country. Her story showed what it was possible to achieve, that Ethiopia's narrative wasn't just one of endless tragedy and failure. That aid works.

Staunchly Christian, Birhan firmly believed that she had survived for a reason. She felt that it was her duty to tell her story on behalf of those people who hadn't survived those dreadful days, those like her mother, Alemetsehay, and sister, Azmera. She was desperate that mass starvation should never again return to Ethiopia.

Birhan knew all about Live Aid as Bisrat had told her about it and shown her the videos. 'I love Bob so much, for what he did with "Do They Know It's Christmas?" and Live Aid. For us famine survivors he is very special. We are so grateful for what he did back in 1984 and what he continues to do now. He's an ambassador for us, for the lives we have endured.' No, she had never met Bob Geldof and she very much doubted that he even knew that she existed.

Then it was time for the photographs. Arthur Edwards has seen and done it all in his near 40-year Fleet Street career. He has photographed nine British Prime Ministers and four US Presidents, two popes and taken some of the most famous pictures of the Queen and Princess Diana. Arthur quickly relaxed Birhan, nattering away to her in his cockney accent. Arthur brings a razor-sharp news sense, a ready wit, and the boundless enthusiasm of an 18 year old to any job. Birhan loved him, rocking with laughter as he implored her to give him 'one of your big, gorgeous smiles'. Arthur would later say it was impossible to take a bad picture of her. The camera loved her and although she was incredibly shy at first, she seemed to enjoy having her photograph taken. Finally, we said goodbye to the family, believing we would never see them again.

Overnighting in the modest Hilltop Hotel outside Mekele, Arthur, Anthony and I set out early the next morning to assess how Ethiopia had changed since Buerk's 1984 reports. On dirt roads in Bisrat's truck we travelled north to Hagere Selam, a village set amid parchment-dry hills scoured grey and dark yellow by the blast-furnace sun. As we pulled up the hope that we had felt after our meeting with Birhan the previous day drained away.

A long, winding queue of ragged, hungry mothers and their crying children was waiting for food aid at a feeding station. A tiny, malnourished child in a filthy blanket stared big-eyed from his mother's arms. Two-year-old Gebreamlake and his mother Medhine, 30, had made an eight-hour, 29km (18 mile) round trip to pick up her monthly 15kg (33lb) handout of wheat. Bisrat translated Medhine's pitiful words. 'We are suffering. I am so worried for Gebreamlake. He is weak with hunger.'

It was awful to witness proud Tigrayans waiting for hand outs to keep them alive. After Band Aid, Live Aid, billions upon billions from Western governments and two decades of hand-wringing, Ethiopians were still going hungry. Six million people would die every year if the West didn't feed them. The appalling scenes of 1984 had not been repeated only because of the country's sophisticated relief network. The population had mushroomed from 42 million in the time of the Great Famine to 70.7 million in 2004. Rains still failed though and Ethiopia still couldn't feed itself.

On October 4 Arthur, Anthony and I flew to Addis for the CFA summit. We were staying in the opulent Sheraton Hotel, a glitzy palace that wouldn't look out of place on Las Vegas's Strip. As we ate in the luxury restaurant it was difficult not to feel a numbing guilt. Addis's expat community is small and gossip rife. Anthony had heard that Geldof had come early to Ethiopia and was in the western Gambela region towards the border with Sudan. What would Geldof say about the scenes we had witnessed in Hagere Selam? I dialled the first hotel listed for Gambela in the Lonely Planet book. Yes, the receptionist said, they did have a Mr Geldof. He went off to fetch him. 'Mr Geldof was in the shower but I told him it was a friend from London'.

'How the fuck did you find me?' Geldof said when he came to the phone. He soon launched into a fiery rant.

'When you go back to Tigray and see feeding stations with, say, 40,000 people and compare it to the million people I saw in 1985, it is progress of a kind. But is it enough? No, it's despicable. The reason we used the pun Band Aid is that you can't put a sticking plaster on a gaping wound. But there is a lack of response from our end politically. Neither *The Sun* nor I should have to keep going on about it but Europe is stuffed with food and the US is stuffed with food.'

Back in London *The Sun*'s Associate Editor Dominic Mohan, now the paper's Editor, rang to tell me how Birhan's interview, which had been published in the paper on October 5, had generated a huge response from readers. Many had phoned and emailed wanting to donate money, just as they had back in 1984. One of the questions I had asked Birhan during our interview was what message she had for Tony Blair.

'We need money for dams and irrigation so our crops don't fail,' the agricultural college student said. 'But we also need money for education, health and to give people jobs. Then we can help ourselves.' Imagine the impact that Birhan's message would have if she could relate the words to him personally. Blair would be in Addis in two days. Why couldn't she tell him face to face?

I called Birhan, who said that she would be delighted to meet Tony Blair. Apart from her family's six-month resettlement by the Derg, she had never left Tigray. We called *The Sun*'s parliamentary lobby team, led by Trevor Kavanagh, to see if Blair would do it. The answer that came back was positive. The interview was to be an exclusive, which would doubtless anger the travelling British press pack who had come all the way from London with the Prime Minister. Geldof also seemed more than happy to take part – especially as he had never met Birhan. Everything seemed to be falling into place.

Then Bisrat called. Every flight from Mekele was booked for the next 24 hours. Even if they started driving now they would never make it in time to meet Blair. In the end, Bisrat used all of his considerable charm and reason with Ethiopia Airlines and miraculously two seats became available.

Arriving at Mekele airport, Birhan had a foreboding sense of dread about getting on an aeroplane, saying, 'My stomach was in my mouth'. The only other time she had flown was the terrifying ride inside the hold of the Antonov two decades before when she and her family were forcibly taken to the Lowlands. It had taken off from this same airstrip. Although a college student in 2004, Birhan was still very much the rural village girl like millions of others across Ethiopia. She knew little of Western life and admits Addis was a complete culture shock. She had been there only once before, passing through on her family's epic 1,300km (800 mile) trek home.

'Everything was crazy and complex in Addis,' she remembers.

'There were so many people and so many cars. It was my first time in a hotel, the first time I had eaten a steak.'

Birhan had decided that Prime Minister Blair should have a present to take home from Ethiopia and so she bought him a 10cm- (4 inch) tall elaborately decorated silver-plaited cross from the holy city of Lalibela. We were driven to the UN building in central Addis and told to wait in a stuffy meeting room away from the main chamber. I sat fiddling anxiously with my tape recorder as we waited. Expecting to spend my time in Ethiopia in clinics and feeding centres, I had failed to bring a suit. Forced to borrow a light grey one from Anthony, I was wearing something that was several sizes too big. Arthur was also looking decidedly nervous.

Birhan was her usual serene self, smiling engagingly. She amused herself by staring out of the closed and soot-stained windows at the batttered blue-and-white Lada taxis honking their horns on the chaotic streets below. Eventually we were told by a smartly groomed aide that the Prime Minister would be a couple more minutes. My mobile rang; it was my boss Dominic. He and his wife, Michelle, had come up with an idea over breakfast that morning. 'Let's ask Geldof to re-record "Do They Know It's Christmas?"' Tell him *The Sun* will back it.' We had no time to dwell on it – Blair and Geldof were being ushered into the room.

The reaction of both men to Birhan was as instantaneous as it was emotional. They had spent the morning in meetings discussing development economics. Now here was Birhan in the flesh. Both were visibly moved. Blair, in particular, looked close to tears. When Birhan handed over the exquisite Lalibela cross to Blair, he told her that he would 'treasure' it and put it above his fireplace when he returned to London. Pausing, Blair added: 'I will see it and it will give me inspiration.' Arthur captured the moment on film.

Blair said that that he remembered seeing Colin Dean's tape at Live Aid: 'It's amazing meeting Birhan now. It brings it all back. It's fantastic she is alive today and doing so well.'

Birhan says that she had heard of Tony Blair before the meeting on October 7, 2004. She thought he was charming, emotional and sincere. Meeting Bob Geldof was far more significant for her though. 'I feel Bob saved my life, it was like, oh God, here is my father.'

As Arthur set up a picture with Blair and Birhan, I cornered a buoyant Geldof. 'Listen Bob, would you re-record "Do They Know It's Christmas?" if *The Sun* gave it a massive push?' Geldof didn't miss a beat. 'If you fucking organize it, I'll do it.' The paper took him at his word.

Dominic, enthused and also moved by Birhan's story, was the former Editor of *The Sun*'s famous 'Bizarre' showbusiness column and had built up impeccable contacts in the pop world. He emailed Chris Martin, from the British band Coldplay.

'Hello Chris... I want to sound you out on something that could be quite special...' The reply soon dropped into Dominic's inbox. 'I'll do it.'

Later Dominic was backstage at one of Scottish chart band Travis's gigs. When asked, lead singer Fran Healy insisted: 'Count me in. I will drop anything to do it, absolutely no question.' Then The Darkness signed up. It was soon clear that this generation of musicians had a conscience.

Dominic called Geldof, now travelling in the Democratic Republic of Congo, and told him that he had secured three of the biggest acts in Britain. 'Congratulations,' he croaked back.

Before leaving Ethiopia I asked Birhan if she would come to London for the re-recording of the single. I told her it would be her chance to explain to the British people and the recording stars just what she had gone through and what the situation in her country was now. I explained that she would be the centre of a lot of media attention and that London would be very different from even Addis. Birhan was eager to tell her story and Bisrat could come along to translate for her.

The Sun announced the project later in October and the cream of Britain's pop artists soon signed up to take part, some of them people who had sung on the original single. Beatle Sir

Paul McCartney, Robbie Williams from chart-topping band Take That and female solo artist Dido whose 1999 album *No Angel* sold 21 million copies worldwide, were participating.

It was decided that the new version of 'Do They Know It's Christmas?' would be recorded at former Beatle's producer Sir George Martin's Air Studios in Hampstead, North London, on November 14, 2004. The 40-strong group of musicians would be known as Band Aid 20. U2 singer Bono would reprise his famous line from the original recording, *'Well, tonight thank God it's them instead of you'.*

Some of the Band Aid 20 members, like pop band The Sugababes and solo artist Will Young, had been at school when the original song was released. Stars like soul singer Joss Stone hadn't even been born. Rapper Dizzee Rascal added a new line, singing: *'You ain't gotta feel guilt, just selfless. Give a little help, to the helpless yo!'*

Among the chorus were stars Katie Melua, Beverley Knight, Ms Dynamite and members of bands Keane and Snow Patrol, who recorded the *'Feed the world'* refrain. Pop band Blur's lead singer Damon Albarn did not sing, but served African cakes and tea instead. It was the same awkward mingling of people as in 1984. Stars who would normally never find themselves in the same place at the same time for a common purpose.

Singer Beverley Knight remembers being worried about whether her fellow stars inside the studio would be 'gossiping and bitching'.

'It wasn't like that at all. Everyone was making cups of tea for each other and stuffing biscuits down their neck, but when it came to the recording everyone was focused on why they were there. The first record was dominated by white males, but this time the gender split is 50–50, and there were lots more artists of colour,' Knight recalls.

Birhan, with Bisrat chaperoning, very nearly didn't make it to the recording at all. *The Sun* had booked them on direct flights from Addis to London, but Bisrat called an hour after they were supposed to be in the air. He explained that they were 'very sorry', but they had spent too much time looking around the terminal at Bole airport and had missed the flight. Re-routed via Dubai, they again missed their connecting flight. 'We were just so amazed by the shops in the airport that we forgot the time,' Birhan recalls. Luckily the airline let them onto the next flight.

The country girl from remote Tigray thought London was 'like going to heaven'. The parks were so green, the soaring buildings more beautiful than she could have imagined. She said Londoners seemed so busy, always hurrying to work. 'In Tigray we always stop people in the street, we love to talk here. In London people don't seem to have the time. When I got back I found it all very difficult to explain to my mother and father. They wouldn't be able to imagine it.'

Birhan especially enjoyed riding on the London Underground network, rattling around from station to station as if it was a fairground ride. She ate food she never dreamt existed – from lobster to traditional British roast beef and Yorkshire pudding. There were visits to London sights like Big Ben and Buckingham Palace that left Birhan wide eyed with amazement.

On the chilly Sunday morning of November 14, banks of photographers were waiting outside Air Studios as Birhan arrived. Birhan and Bisrat emerged from a people carrier with dark, tinted windows and were led unnoticed to a little backroom inside the studio. Geldof gathered the 40-odd stars together before recording began. He wanted to show the young stars, many barely old enough to remember Michael Buerk's reports, why they were there. He had set up a video screen and ran Colin Dean's heart-wrenching Live Aid tape. Britain's biggest pop stars were numbed into silence.

As the video reached Birhan's wasted features Geldof stopped the tape. He motioned to a nearby door to a side room and out walked Birhan. Geldof told the throng of stars: 'This beautiful and intelligent woman and thousands of others like her are here today because of what Band Aid did 20 years ago.'

Soul singer Joss Stone began to weep and the young girls in the Sugababes broke down too. Singer Natasha Bedingfield said: 'I don't think there was a dry eye in the room. Seeing someone who had been so close to death looking so healthy made me realize that doing this can really help people.' It was a piece of showmanship Geldof would later repeat to great dramatic effect at Live 8.

Birhan was delighted to meet Geldof's daughter, Pixie, who wore the same 'Feed the World' T-shirt that her father had worn at the recording 20 years previously. Birhan posed for endless photographs but she didn't mind. 'I was used to the cameras by now,' she says.

As the recording came to an end Birhan was asked what she would like to do now. Go to a decent restaurant perhaps? Or a visit to the theatre? She replied, 'Could I have another ride on the Tube trains? It's so much fun.'

The single sold 72,000 copies in just 24 hours when it was released on November 29, 2004, and went straight to Number One in the UK charts. It became the biggest-selling single of 2004, as well as the Christmas Number One and raised £3 million for people in the war-torn Darfur region of Sudan as well as Ethiopia. A new generation had taken on Band Aid's mantle. Africa was back at the top of the political agenda. It was the conversation down the pub and in the work place.

Geldof underlined that the new record was about justice not charity: that a pop record, and those that bought it, and pop singers couldn't beat global poverty. Politicians, however, could. He wanted the buying of the single to be a political statement so that when Tony Blair met the world's richest leaders at the G8 conference in Britain the following summer he would push to make sure children no longer went to bed hungry across Africa every night. Birhan, who had appeared in the song's video, was now a globally recognized face. She coped with all the attention with amazing maturity and level-headedness. She explained that after surviving the famine she felt this was her destiny.

Then David Stables called. Birhan had been asked to appear on the *Oprah Winfrey Show*, along with Brian Stewart. Birhan's fame had spread far and wide. Oprah Winfrey was the most famous chatshow host in the world – 62 million viewers had watched her interview with African American pop star Michael Jackson alone. It would be a huge opportunity to spread the Band Aid 20 message. Birhan and Bisrat flew to Chicago from London and joined Stewart in the show's stretch limo on the way to the taping. 'Before the show I had a case of nerves. Birhan none at all,' Stewart now remembers.

Oprah told Birhan: 'You are a miracle.' Birhan mesmerized the audience telling of her life commitment to help suffering children as she had been helped with such compassion two decades earlier. Birhan and Stewart sat in the audience for another portion of the show. When they left during a commercial break the audience rose to give her a standing ovation, the only time the show's producers had seen such a reaction for a guest.

When Birhan returned to Tigray and her studies no one in Kwiha had heard about the new 'Do They Know It's Christmas?' single or the *Oprah Winfrey Show*.

Her father Woldu asked Birhan: '*Who is Tony Blair?*'

Geldof was unequivocal when asked about a Live Aid 2 by Bono. He thought it was a bad idea. When his old friend from Dublin pleaded with him, Geldof blurted out: 'You fucking do it then.' The CFA had reported with clear recommendations for debt relief in the poorest countries, increasing aid packages and fairer trade. That was enough for Geldof. Yet, as the weeks and months of 2005 rolled on Geldof became increasingly frustrated. World leaders didn't seem to be responding to the CFA's demands. The proposed July meeting of G8 leaders at Gleneagles in Scotland, almost 20 years to the week that Live Aid had stopped the world, was creeping closer but a new deal for Africa seemed to be slipping away.

Richard Curtis, the comedy writer of movie hits such as *Four Weddings and a Funeral*, was a founder of British charity Comic Relief. He was now supporting Make Poverty History, an alliance of charities, unions and campaign groups, and believed a new Live Aid was the best way to persuade G8 leaders to meet the activists' demands on Africa. The United States and other rich nations were dragging their feet on the CFA's recommendations on debt relief and increased aid. But finally, Geldof was warming to the idea of another concert. 'We'll make it justice, not charity: we don't want your money, we want you.'

In April 2005, U2's Bono, Geldof and Midge Ure, the former Ultravox singer and co-organizer of Live Aid, met with Curtis in his London office. Harvey Goldsmith, the promoter of Live Aid, was also present. They were there to discuss whether a concert was possible. Geldof began calling his friends in the music world to see if they would take part. By early May he thought he could do it. 'I had three names on a piece of paper – McCartney, U2 and Coldplay,' he says. 'I had no venue, no broadcaster, no organizational infrastructure but I took those three names home and decided I was going to do this.' Other names, such as Madonna and Sting, were added even before Geldof had asked them because he was confident they would perform.

On May 8 Geldof rang publicist Bernard Doherty, his old friend and Live Aid collaborator. 'You are in, mate, whether you fucking like it or not – and I'm not paying you.' A similar call to Goldsmith alerted the producer to look for venues. Goldsmith called promoters in France, Germany, Italy and the US to get things going there. Finally on May 31 Curtis and Geldof announced that Live 8 was going ahead and that it would be 'the greatest show on Earth'. Pink Floyd would re-form for the event, as would The Who. Sir Elton John would play with rising star Pete Doherty. It was going to be phenomenal.

I rang Tigray and asked Birhan if she could come over to London once again. I explained the significance of the occasion. Birhan was desperate to come and would be accompanied by Bisrat and his girlfriend, Rahel. Even then, Birhan couldn't possibly have imagined the magnitude of Live 8. Few could have. Only when she was standing on the huge Live 8 stage, her dark fingers entwined with superstar Madonna's and raised in triumph could it possibly have hit home. That is one of the defining images of the decade. The 205,000 people gathered in Hyde Park and the billions watching on TV across the globe had heard over and over that every day, somewhere in the world, 50,000 people die from illnesses that could easily be prevented. Every day.

When Geldof introduced Birhan as she stood in front of her own frozen, emaciated image from the 1984 Colin Dean video it made the statistics come alive. It showed the importance of one life saved. This one woman brimmed over with potential and the beauty of humanity. 'Don't let them tell you this doesn't work,' was Geldof's comment from the stage.

That image was enough to move George W. Bush, the world's most powerful man. Even Birhan's friends in remote Kwiha in Tigray's faraway mountains saw her. Her little sister Silas watched her sister on a flickering TV screen at the family's stone cottage. 'We were all in tears. She was so brave, we were so proud of her,' Silas said. Her father missed the moment: Woldu was busy with his cattle outside.

Despite everything, Birhan was unmoved by the adulation that followed: 'I had witnessed too many bad things. My mother and sister had died in the famine. I didn't want other families to suffer like I once had.'

After Live 8, the eyes of the world were on the luxury Scottish hotel of Gleneagles, where the G8 leaders were meeting from July 6 to 8. Geldof had the mandate of billions of Live 8 viewers in his pocket. 'Politics is numbers. Tony Blair will go to a five-star hotel on a golf course next week and say to seven other guys, "I come with the largest democratic mandate ever collected in the history of this planet".'

The Sun arranged for Birhan to travel north and stay at the baronial Atholl Palace Hotel in Pitlochry, amid glorious Highland scenery. Arthur Edward's ginger-haired son Paul, also a *Sun* photographer, was this time taking the pictures. The young Ethiopians greatly enjoyed their slice of Scottish life. Ever-dapper Bisrat decided he would like to try on a kilt and a traditional Tam-o'-Shanter tartan cap. Much to Birhan's delight, he then stood under a stuffed stag's head in the hotel bar to down a dram of the finest malt whisky. Birhan tried a round of golf for the first time, while her white traditional Ethiopian shawl flapped in the Highland breeze. And she also wrote an open letter to the G8 leaders saying: 'Live 8 was supported by millions. The politicians now have to listen to their people. I will continue my prayers to God to give the eight leaders soft hearts. This is a historical moment when Africa can be changed.'

Britain was euphoric on July 6. London, it was announced, would hold the 2012 Olympic Games. Birhan was also jubilant, wondering if world-famous Ethiopian long distance runner Haile Gebrselassie would take part in the games. But the following day the celebrations were crushed. On what was to become known as 7/7, in a blaze of twisted metal and white light suicide bombers struck London, killing 54 and injuring around 700. Birhan said she would pray for the bereaved.

On July 8, we decided to return to London, driving the long-haul down the arterial M1 motorway. My mobile rang while we were taking a toilet break. It was a euphoric Geldof. The G8 leaders had agreed to boost aid for developing countries by US $50 billion, but that was not all. They had also endorsed a deal agreed before the summit by their finance ministers to write off US $40 million of debt owed by the 18 poorest countries in the world. On trade, there was a commitment to work towards cutting subsidies and tariffs.

'It's a great day,' Geldof said. 'We estimate as a result of what happened today 10 million more Africans will be alive in 2010. That's 10 million more like Birhan.' He said the agreements were 'a great riposte' to the terrorist outrages in London, adding: 'It is the world fighting back as a force for good.'

UN Secretary General Kofi Annan called the G8 meeting 'the greatest summit for Africa ever'.

U2 singer Bono said: 'Does it end extreme poverty? No. Is it a great start? Yes.'

When Birhan was told, she smiled to herself. The world had listened.

'If my story has inspired people then I'm very proud and honoured,' she said, before adding, 'I'm *so* glad Bob is happy.'

OUT OF THE DARKNESS, INTO THE LIGHT

AFTER LECTURES at her agricultural college in the little Tigrayan town of Wukro Birhan would meet her friend Birhanu Meresa for a dark *bune* coffee. The pungent smell of cattle hides being processed at the nearby Sheba Tannery wafted over the town as they nattered away. Their laughter filled the chill evening mountain air as goats and donkeys laden with firewood or charcoal were driven through the streets by the owners returning from market to their little farmsteads in the brown hills around the town. The pair were 'like brother and sister'. Sometimes they would visit the churches carved into stone rock faces on the fringes of the dusty low-rise town of stone shacks and concrete municipal buildings an 80-minute bus ride north of Mekele. Both were devout Christians and the couple had become close.

Birhan's best friend at college, Alamnesh, was thrilled. 'Birhanu is the male Birhan,' she told her. In the coffee bars in the evening Birhan, Birhanu and Alemnesh would listen to the wandering Azmari musicians playing their one-stringed wooden instrument with a gut-string bow, making up the words to their songs as they went along like an American rapper. The students danced the traditional way, rolling their shoulders and jutting their necks in rhythm with the music.

Birhan, who had returned from the Live 8 concert in the summer of 2005, more determined than ever to do well in her studies, felt able to talk to Birhanu about anything. He helped her make sense of what she had been through. The famine, the loss of her mother and sister, being the little child among the thousands that the camera had focused on.

They also had so much in common. There was his name *Birhanu*, the male version of Birhan's name meaning 'light'. He also had a rural farming background and tragedy had haunted his past. Like Birhan, there were the mental scars of the 1984 famine. 'I knew the pain he had gone through during the famine because I went through it too,' she emphasizes.

A handsome man, Birhan also carried the scars of his past on his left cheek and in the missing tip of his left ear. Born around 1981, Birhanu is the eldest of five boys who grew up in the same grinding and precarious subsistence farming life as Birhan. His home village is in southern Tigray in the small village of Raya Azebo, 15km (9 miles) south of the town of Maychew.

Birhanu's family was rich before the 1984 famine. His father, Meresa, and mother, Zewdu, owned a large herd of 26 cattle and grew lush fields of *tef*, the staple grain of *injera* bread, as well as sorghum and maize.

When Birhanu was an eight-month-old baby, he was left in the care of some older boys while his father was out with the cattle and his mother on a three-hour round trip to fetch water from the river. The eight-year-old boy who was cradling him, accidentally dropped him into a roaring log fire. The boys ran away and left Birhanu screaming in pain among the burning logs. 'By the will of God one of the boys returned and pulled me from the fire,' Birhanu says in his very good English. 'He threw me on the ground to put out where my face was burning. It had roasted my face.'

Meresa returned from the fields screaming: 'What's happened to my child?' Birhanu's father then ran 10km (6 miles) with him to a clinic to get help. Later the burn on the left side of his face became infected and began weeping pus. Birhanu was forced to sleep on the right side of his head as the burn slowly healed. 'The eagles had been circling in the sky. I was wounded and damaged but God saved me,' he says.

Like Birhan he grew up herding goats and cattle. In 1984 the Great Famine swept through Raya Azebo devastating crops and leaving their livestock weak and dying. 'It was unbelievable, like a terrible dream. The famine devastated us; we had no cattle left, we were begging but no one else had any food either. No *injera*, no stew,' he adds.

Many starving families from the area migrated to Sudan where there was food aid but Birhanu's mother didn't want to go. So Birhanu, his mother, Zewdu, and brother, Haftu, were left to share a single cup of roasted wheat with added salt between them each day. They slumped listlessly in their *sekela* hut for most of the day, praying for salvation. They didn't have the strength to do anything else. They went to their ox skin bed hungry every night for 10 months. It was this shared horror which bound Birhanu and Birhan together.

The family was saved by food aid from the West, possibly as a result of Band Aid. There was milk powder, cooking oil, even clothes. Birhanu didn't start school until he was 15, but he was a strong pupil and later went on to Wukro Agricultural College. It was here that he was introduced by friends to Birhan in 2004 and where he found out that they had so much in common and so much to talk about. He told her: 'I don't have a sister, promise me you will be my sister'. He also watched Birhan with Madonna at Live 8 on TV at his uncle's house. 'I was very proud. She was so brave. It was wonderful. The whole world was listening as she spoke in the Tigrinya language. I was inspired.'

In the summer of 2006 Birhan graduated in plant science with decent grades and a burning ambition to work to improve her homeland. She won a place at Mekele's Sheba University to study nursing. Her childhood dream had come true. It should have been a joyous moment for Birhan but there was more tears and gut-wrenching sadness. Her best friend Alamnesh was due to graduate at the same time. She and Birhan had already posed for a photograph in their black gowns and mortar board hats in anticipation of the event. But Birhan had received a call from Alamnesh's family. Her great friend had been taken ill suddenly and died from a 'fever'. Although locals blamed the illness on bats, which they said had urinated on Alemnesh thus spreading disease, it is more likely that malaria was the cause.

Birhan wept and wept and prayed to the Lord. 'I was never so sad as that. Alemnesh was like my sister. She was only 24. It crushed me. We had started out learning Plant Science together. Every weekend I would either cook for her or she would cook for me. We loved to dance to Tigrayan music together. Now she was gone. I couldn't believe it.'

By the August of 2006 grieving Birhan was globetrotting once more. With her friend, Rahel, Bisrat's girlfriend, she flew to Toronto to stay for a month with Brian Stewart and his family. The highlight for the Ethiopians was being drenched on a ferry ride beneath Niagara Falls. Dripping with the misty water droplets, Birhan said it 'felt like a second baptism'. She loved spending time with the journalist, his wife, Tina, and daughter, Katie, but she realized that she missed Birhanu and their long conversations peppered with laughter. Perhaps there was more to her feelings for him after all than just a platonic friendship? After spending nearly a month in Canada she knew that she didn't want to live outside her beloved Ethiopia. She wanted to stay in Tigray and help rebuild her country.

Back in Mekele that autumn Birhan threw herself into university life. She rented a small and modest flat with her half-sister, Medhine, near the centre of the city and devoted herself to her nursing studies. Her sometimes chronic shyness from earlier years, especially around *farenjis*, had well and truly gone. 'The whole Live 8 experience gave me so much confidence,' she admits. 'I had spoken to billions on that stage. Nothing felt too daunting after that.' Her English, after much hard work, was improving too.

University lecturer Nigusse Kidane Mariam, who taught Birhan epidemiology, says. 'In our culture if you have a problem you often stay quiet. People think that if they ask a question the others might laugh at them. Birhan is not like that. She was a conscientious student. She was so interested, which is something teachers love.' He said that Birhan was incredibly self-effacing and didn't make a big deal of her huge contribution to both Band Aid 20 and Live 8.

Fellow trainee nurse Selam Getachew became a close friend. They went out for meals of *injera* or pizza, watched English Premiership football, which is wildly popular in Ethiopia and danced to traditional Tigrayan music. 'Selam is very extrovert and very beautiful,' Birhan says. 'We have no secrets, we go shopping, we talk about relationships.'

Birhan told Selam all about Birhanu. How his life resonated with hers. It seemed Birhanu felt the same and in 2007 he told Birhan that he loved her. He says today: 'When she is happy, I'm happy. When she is angry, I am angry. We are like the same person. We need each other.'

That summer Birhan went to visit Birhanu's family at their home village in the Lowlands of Tigray south of Maychew.

The young couple had a wonderful time dining with relatives and walking in the grassy, low hills. It was blazing hot, dark clouds of insects swarmed everywhere. A few days later Birhan woke up in the tiny Mekele flat that she shared with Medhine with her bed sheets wet with sweat. Her head was thumping like a drum, the muscles in her thighs and arms were aching sharply. She flung off the bed sheets to get some cool air and within seconds she was shivering with cold. Later her temperature had soared to over 38°C (100.4°F).

'I was boiling hot, I couldn't eat, I was shaking violently,' she says, her neat features screwing up at the thought. Birhan knew what it was like to be on the edge of death. She knew she was very ill and following her nursing training she recognized the symptoms. She had been struck down by another of Africa's deadly killers, malaria, which claims the lives of more young children than any other single disease. Worldwide, malaria causes around 225 million illnesses and 781,000 deaths annually.

A doctor was hurriedly sent for and tests done. The potentially fatal disease was confirmed as the cause of her illness and she was quickly given medication.

Birhan must have been bitten by a mosquito in the Lowlands while visiting Birhanu's family. The mountains around Mekele are too high for the insects. Birhanu was beside himself with worry. He stayed with her night and day as she battled her way back to health. It would take another week with Birhan lying exhausted in bed before she was able to get to her feet again.

She was soon back at college studying hard and was able to graduate from university in nursing in the summer of 2009. It was one of the proudest moments of Birhan's life. She had achieved what she had dreamed of since she was a little girl and what had once seemed so impossible. She began assisting at a clinic in Mekele, helping assess sick and malnourished children. She loved the work – it was all she had ever wanted to do, but like many recent graduates across the globe she struggled to find full-time work. Then later that year Bob Geldof came back to Ethiopia.

It was November 2009, 25 years after 'Do They Know It's Christmas?' was first released and Geldof was back in Mekele. He had returned to see how Band Aid and Live Aid's money had been spent. In that year at least 6 million of the now 85 million-strong Ethiopian population were in need of food aid to keep them alive after three years of poor rains. All these years later and Ethiopia still couldn't feed itself.

Naysayers in the British press had asked whether Band Aid's efforts had achieved very much at all. At Live 8 Geldof had told his critics: 'I am withering in my scorn for those who say it's not going to work. Even if it doesn't work, what do they propose? Every night forever watching people dying on our TV screens?' Now back in the Ethiopian Highlands Geldof was profoundly moved by what he saw.

In Addis and Mekele there was a construction boom with high-rise housing blocks and factories springing up. A massive road-building programme was underway. Elsewhere power stations, dams and hydroelectric plants were being built, much of it with billions in Chinese investment. The nation now had 23 universities. The entrepreneurial spirit was flourishing and banks booming. The gross domestic product (GDP) – from a pitifully low level – had grown by an average of 11 percent per annum in the seven years to 2010.

The battle against poverty is being slowly won and Ethiopia is rising. Close to 49.5 percent of the total population were under the poverty line in 1994–95 but that is believed to have declined to 29.2 percent in 2009–10. The under-five mortality rate has decreased from 167 per 1,000 in 2001–02 to 101 per 1000 in 2009–10. Malaria cases had also dropped by two-thirds between 2006 and 2009, with the number of deaths halved thanks to the spraying of one million houses and the distribution of 20 million bed nets, allowing people like Birhan to survive. Throughout Ethiopia the numbers of children in school have trebled between the 1984 famine and 2009 when 71 percent of children were in education. This is not just the result of aid, but also the fruit of the campaigning to drop the debt. Ethiopia's annual interest on debt was slashed from US $195m in 2001 to US $86m in 2007. That extra money has gone into schools and hospitals. Geldof says: 'As a result of what was done on debt at Gleneagles and elsewhere 37 million more children are in school. So much for aid not working.'

Geldof was further reassured in a two-hour private meeting with Ethiopian Prime Minister Meles Zenawi that the 'biblical' famine of 1984 would not be repeated.

'We've put in systems to alert us to that and mechanisms to reverse the problems that led to it,' Meles insisted. 'We've had several droughts but no famine over the past 18 years.'

He had instituted a Safety Net programme in case of crop failure, which in 2005 gave food to 7.6 million people in return for labour on public works like road maintenance and tree planting. Around 8 percent of the population relies on food aid, compared with more than double that percentage in 1985.

Meles insisted that to say nothing had changed in Ethiopia since 1984 'is not just a lie, it is also disempowering… It implies that all the efforts in the meantime have been useless – and that leads to paralysis rather than action. Many people are working their hearts out, and they have made real progress – not enough perhaps – but real progress.'

Geldof set off for Tigray to see what difference Band Aid money had made on the ground. Nestled in a natural mountain amphitheatre around an hour's drive north of Mekele, the Hagere Selam School, which had been built with £85,000 of Band Aid cash and run by the A-CET charity, provides an education for 500 children. Geldof's Toyota Land Cruiser pulled up on the rocky track outside the stone school buildings. He pushed through a crowd of ululating women and watched three little boys squinting in the sun as they tended their herd of sweeping-horned cattle.

He found a welcoming committee awaiting him. Birhan, in her brilliant white *shamma* shawl, her hair plated in the Tigray tradition, ran forward to greet him. The last time they had met was Live 8. They hugged tightly and Birhan buried her face in his chest. Arthur Edwards and I were also there to capture the moment for *The Sun*.

Then Geldof greeted the rest of the party. First Claire Berstchinger, the Red Cross nurse from Michael Buerk's original BBC reports from the 1984 famine. A practicing Buddhist for many years, Bertschinger had come to terms with the trauma she suffered during the famine. She had been appointed director of tropical nursing at the London School of Hygiene and Tropical Medicine and a trustee and ambassador for A-CET. Next Geldof saw Bisrat Mesfin, grinning from ear to ear. 'Ah the dude who danced with Madonna in front of billions,' Geldof smiled. Geldof gratefully accepted an A-CET baseball cap from Bisrat and pulled it over his greying, straggly hair. Then came A-CET's founder and Bisrat's mentor David Stables. The ex-military man looked close to tears. Geldof was a long-time hero.

The group strolled between ranks of smiling children aged 7 to 15 all wearing white A-CET T-shirts. Inside the airy classrooms children sat at desks rather than on the floor, their books and equipment just like that found in Western schools. After a while, the party went outside the red-roofed solid stone buildings to where a local band of musicians in bright white smocks and red embroidered waistcoats had set up their instruments on a wobbly wooden stage. Banners proclaimed,

'*Education is the key to success*' and '*We are making poverty history*'.

As Geldof and the rest took their seats on fold-up plastic chairs the band began to play. The loudspeakers were old and rickety and the wind had got up somewhat but the tune was unmistakeable. '*It's Christmas time and there's no need to be afraid...*' Geldof's eyes moistened. 'It's better than the real thing,' he yelled. He added: 'As a result of what Gleneagles did on debt 37 million more children are in school. And 500 of those are here in this school.'

As the Band Aid song continued through the distorted speakers, Birhan felt so proud and delighted at the children's smiling faces. Fiercely proud of Ethiopia, she leant over and said softly: 'See what education can do for us. Life is like a road which has opened up everything for me thanks to school and college. It is full of possibilities. Bob is a hero to me and so many famine survivors here.'

The following day, after Geldof's party had left, Birhan took Claire Bertschinger to Mekele Health Centre where she had been volunteering. Her deep empathy with the children was touching. Bertschinger was impressed how Birhan and her generation of famine survivors were turning around the country. 'The place is thriving,' she said. 'There are good roads, new factories, a busy university and local people in the restaurants. There have been two years of consecutive droughts but the famine early warning systems are now working well. People look healthy, children are well, livestock look good. There are certain areas of food shortages that need addressing but overall I'm very positive.'

As her country changes, so Birhan's own life moves on. Birhanu, who had been driving a blue auto rickshaw taxi around Mekele's streets to make ends meet while he studied at college, eventually saved a little bit of money, enough so that he could ask Birhan if she would be his wife. She wept tears of joy, saying she 'loved him very much'. After so many years of pain Birhan had now discovered profound happiness.

In January 2010, Birhan and Birhanu had a 'ring ceremony', a sort of engagement, which allowed their respective families to meet and get to know each other. Dressed in a white gown and veil, Birhan exchanged rings with her fiancé and received a blessing from a priest in Kwiha. Birhanu was 'overjoyed' adding: 'Birhan is frank with her love, she's kind and honest. I don't have the words to express my love for her.' One day if they have the funds the couple might have a big wedding although it's not a necessity in their culture.

Birhan and Birhanu moved into a two-roomed stone house in the centre of Mekele, sharing a dusty yard with another family. It seemed that Birhan's luck was changing. She had more good news. She was offered a well-paid job with the UN's World Food Programme (WFP) as a Food Monitor Assistant. Her dreams were coming true.

As part of her job she travels to remote villages assessing if children are malnourished or suffering from disease. Birhan clearly adores her work. She weighs and measures the children and those found to be too thin are given a supplementary food of enriched peanut butter paste. It does not need mixing with water, which might not be clean, as was the case in 1984. She also educates villagers on nutrition and HIV. After trips out into the field Birhan then inputs her findings back at the WFP's computer database. 'The children need help, they can't help themselves. The job goes with my history and it's what I enjoy,' she says.

In her second-storey office on the outskirts of Mekele, the head of the WFP's local sub-office Mei Liu says: 'Birhan's attitude is to learn and do more. She loves working with children.'

WFP staff assistant mother-of-two Genet Bekuretsion has become good friends with Birhan and describes her as 'a miracle'. She adds: 'Birhan is evidence for us that there was some salvation from the terrible famine times. It is wonderful that she is helping others.'

Birhan feels that her life has come full circle. She says that she loves helping others as she was once helped by aid workers and medics herself. She uses her knowledge of both agriculture and medicine on her field visits with WFP.

Birhanu says: 'She loves children and helping them; that's how she wants to spend her life.'

Now the couple are praying for children of their own. 'I want a little boy and a little girl,' Birhan says. 'I'm praying for a child this year.

'It would make my life complete.'

EPILOGUE

IT IS CHRISTMAS EVE and Birhan and Birhanu are shopping for a goat. Parking Birhanu's blue-and-white tuk-tuk – a motorized rickshaw – at Mekele's livestock market they move through the bleating herds, expertly running their hands down each goat's back as they assess its value for money. There are several hundred goats on the dustbowl patch of ground the size of two football pitches. The couple are looking for a last-minute Christmas bargain though.

The blazing midday sun is intense; the east wind whips up fine yellow dust, spraying it into the eyes, noses and mouths of those around. Farmers from the mountains, swathed in brilliant white *gabi* shawls, their *dula* sticks flexed over their shoulders, stand beside their lop-eared goats, trying to strike a hard bargain with those looking for a seasonal feast. Each wizened seller, most wearing turbans to ward off the scorching heat, seems to have fewer teeth than the last.

Finally the couple find what they've been searching for, a tawny-haired nanny with strong haunches and broad shoulders. And so, the haggling begins. After much tortured pleading and gesticulating Birhanu strikes a deal for 500 birr. 'It's a fair price. The goat will last us,' he reassures.

The nanny is dragged by a length of rope to a waiting tuk-tuk by an elderly, toothless market worker for a one birr tip. The driver then follows Birhanu's tuk-tuk back over the bone-jarring unpaved roads to the couple's little square-stoned, two-roomed home. The goat is tethered in the yard and given some olive branches to munch on. It is its last supper. It will be slaughtered by Birhanu in the morning.

Inside the neat home, the bedroom doubles as the living room. Medieval-style icons of St George slaying the dragon and Mary with the baby Jesus hang from the walls. There are two sturdy armchairs, a little TV and a fridge. Birhan makes *bune*. The charcoal glows in the little tin brazier as she wafts the pungent incense in the gloom of the cottage. She explains that the best Ethiopia coffee grows wild and is sown by the birds. It is so much better than that planted by man.

Birhanu has prepared a lunch of tasty Ethiopian honey with crisp bread, roasted barley, groundnuts and locally grown oranges. Both he and Birhan have the reverence for food that those who have known desperate hunger often share.

Birhanu, who graduates in disaster relief and sustainable development in the summer of 2011, expertly slices open an orange with a little Stanley knife and says quietly: 'This is what we need more of. We need to feed ourself.' Warming to the topic, he adds: 'We have huge natural resources, especially in agriculture, but have to harness them better. We have a lot of groundwater, a lot of rainwater and need to utilize it better. People here are good farmers, we still have excess land, we need technical help from overseas to make the land better.'

Birhan, dressed in tight blue jeans, black canvas plimsolls and a tight blue jumper, nods her head in agreement. 'We

Ethiopians are so proud of our country,' she says thoughtfully. 'We have such a rich culture but we are still known in other countries for famine. We must never forget those who died like my mother and sister and never let such a disastrous situation happen again. Ethiopia is a different place now though, things are developing very quickly.'

The *bune* is rich and sugary, a supercharged boost after the third cup. Birhan, the one-time country girl, now loves city life. She has recently passed her driving test at the first attempt and she hopes to one day buy a car and own her own house, big enough for the children she wants to have with Birhanu.

The couple eat out at trendy restaurants like the Boston in the centre of Mekele, which serves cream cakes and tiramisu. Like most people in Ethiopia, they are avid fans of English Premiership football, which is shown on TV. Birhan supports 'Manchi', Manchester United, and likes striker Wayne Rooney's skill in front of the goal.

Today Birhan incorporates Western culture with the old Ethiopian way of life. She enjoys listening to Celine Dion and Shakira but is equally happy playing traditional Tigrayan church music. That Christmas Eve night Mekele hums along to the sound of prayer. Amplified by loudspeakers, the rhythmic chanting echoes in the darkness. The next morning finds Birhan dressed in a brilliant white tunic with her *shamma* shawl draped carefully around her shoulders. Her hair is plaited in neat cornrows – apparently in the Tigrayan style. Birhanu laughs at this: 'Her hair is not completely traditional you know. That's a modern style.'

The couple's first stop on this Christmas morning – January 7, 2011 in the Western calendar – is at a large hall near the Axum Hotel in Mekele's centre. Bisrat and his local organization EYES, which is linked to A-CET, are laying on a Christmas feast for the local street children of *tibbs*, sliced lamb pan-fried in butter, and *injera* bread. Everyone eats in the traditional way with their right hand without cutlery. The youngsters crowd around Birhan, as she clucks at them to be good and finish their food.

Then it is back to Birhanu's tuk-tuk. With the goat meat wrapped in brown paper and a large cream cake on her lap, Birhan sits in the back as Birhanu revs the engine and swings away onto the main road out of town. On the left they pass the new chrome-and-plastic-seated Texas burger bar. The tuk-tuk splutters and strains to make it up the steep hill out of Mekele past the cement and tile factories and new blocks of flats. Soon they pass wisps of people in turbans with chickens dangling on strings from either side of their *dula* sticks, as they drive their firewood-laden donkeys before them on the windswept plateau. On their right they pass the place where the camp was located in which Woldu spent Christmas Day 1984 alone, surviving on just a single bread roll. Next they see the airstrip, where the old Antonov was loaded with Birhan's family and dozens of other Tigrayan farmers to resettle them forcibly in the Lowlands.

In a few minutes giant white wind turbines come into view on the horizon. They are near the village of Ashegoda. Ethiopia is really changing, it seems. Now the tuk-tuk climbs towards Kwiha, Birhan's childhood hometown, with the huge silver dome of St Mary's Church towering over the stone and tin shacks. In another time this was a place associated with mass starvation and death, but now there is life.

Pulling up outside her family's welcoming compound, Birhan sees Woldu as he rushes out through the yellow iron gates to welcome his daughter and her fiancé. They walk past the cow dung drying on the stone walls, ignoring the two severed goats' heads lying in the dust in the yard.

Inside the modest cottage, a Christmas tree made of a few conifer branches is decorated with different-coloured balloons and blue flashing fairy lights. Religious icons and *injera* baskets line the walls. Brian Stewart's photo still has pride of place on the mantelpiece. Woldu says a prayer, finishing with: 'And God bless us not to see famine in this country.'

Letebirhan then brings in a huge plate of *injera* as a shared platter. The family tear off pieces of the pancake-like bread to scoop up the spicy *wat* stew of chickpeas and goat. There are big, frothy mugs of home-brewed *tella* beer, more *bune* and popcorn. Then a DVD of traditional Tigrayan dancing is put into the crackling TV on the dresser. Everyone is swaying, gyrating their shoulders and clapping along to the music. Woldu clutches his mug of *tella*, his eyes rheumy as he squints at the television.

The old patriarch wears the contented smile of an African father, one surrounded by his extended family – and a toddler who has wandered in from next door to listen to the music.

Of Woldu's eight children only Lemlem is not present. She is at home in their ancestral village of Lahama. When the prickly pear cactus fruit ripen Birhan will go back there to see her sister. She will sleep on ox skins on the cold earth like she did as a child. Lemlem has a different life. She married young and didn't have the same chance of education as Birhan and Silas. Her life is a more traditional one, one of back-breaking toil in the fields with her brood of children. There is no electricity, TV or running water where she lives. Mekele may have burger bars, tile factories and internet cafes; there may even be wind turbines, but out in rural Ethiopia, the old way of life still exists and it seems as if little has changed since the Iron Age.

In a flowing light blue robe, little Silas, now aged 28, dances rhythmically with big sister, Birhan, to the Arabic-tinged music. Woldu smiles contentedly at the healthy-looking girls whom he carried around 1,300 km (800 miles) on his shoulders from the Lowlands when they were tiny. They are now both radiantly beautiful and educated women. Unmarried Silas is a secretary for the government's Urban Development Office in Kwiha. She wants to take a master's degree in management.

Woldu's moist eyes appear to flicker with the flames from the charcoal of the coffee brazier. 'I feel so honoured because of what Birhan has achieved.' He scratches his grizzled beard. 'She wants to help others – which is what God wants.'

Later Birhanu kick-starts the tuk-tuk and he and Birhan roar back down the hill away from the family home towards Mekele. Birhan now seems to be lost in reverie, but on her face is a wide beaming smile. The orange sun begins to dip under the Tigrayan mountains. It casts a blinding, luminous glow across the plateau. There is no darkness here now. Everything only seems bathed in light.

***

PUBLISHER'S NOTE

As this book goes to press, famine in East Africa has once again hit the world's headlines. Severe drought has resulted in a massive food crisis – the worst in 60 years – in Somalia, Ethiopia, Kenya and other countries in the Horn of Africa. As of July 2011, an estimated 10,000 people have died of starvation. Without aid, a further 12 million people are at risk of death, according to the UN. New Holland Publishers are donating proceeds from the sale of this book to Oxfam's DEC East Africa Crisis Appeal, which provides life-saving clean water, food and other emergency aid to those affected. If you would like to make a similar donation please go to the Oxfam website: www.oxfam.org.uk

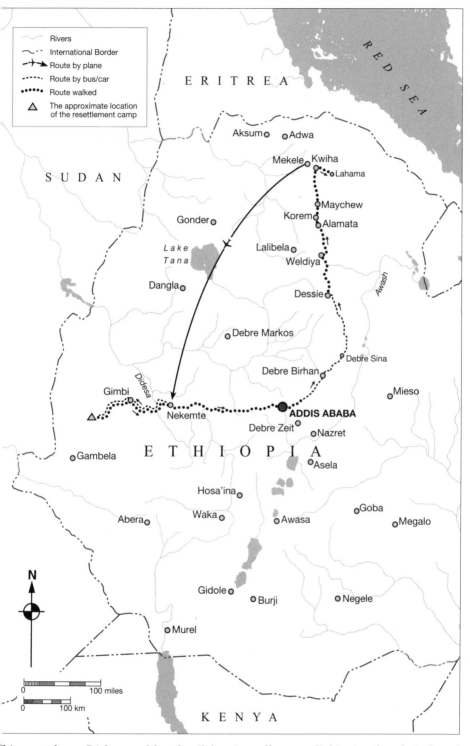

This map shows Birhan and her family's epic walk across Ethiopia after their forced settlement in the Lowlands in 1985. Birhan's father, Woldu, carried his daughters, Birhan and Silas, on his shoulders for more than 900km (560 miles).

GLOSSARY

A-CET – African Children's Education Trust

Amharic – national language of Ethiopia

Azmari – traditional wandering singer and musician

Baraka – third cup of coffee drunk during the Ethiopian coffee ceremony. Known as the blessing cup

Birr – Ethiopian currency. One birr is made up of 100 cents. US dollar = *c*.17 birr; UK pound = *c*.27 at the time of writing.

Belg – 'small' rains in March/April

Buda – spirit that can possess people

Bune or *buna* – coffee

CFA – Commission for Africa

Derg – from the Ge'ez word meaning 'committee', Communist junta that governed Ethiopia under Colonel Mengistu Haile Mariam between 1974 and 1991

Dula – hardwood stick used by travelling Highlanders to herd cattle, carry loads to and from market and brace the shoulders during long treks

Farenji – foreigner

Gabi – thick blanket of woven cotton, usually white, wrapped around the shoulders

Ge'ez – ancient Semitic language

which is the root of both Tigrinya and Amharic. No longer spoken, it survives as the language used in Ethiopian church services

Hidmo – stone homestead

Injera – grey flatbread resembling a large pancake

Meher – 'big' rains that take place from June to September

Mogogo – large black clay plate placed over a fire to cook injera

NGO – non-governmental organization

Relief and Rehabilitation Commission (RRC) – Ethiopian government agency set up after the 1973 drought

Sekela – traditional cone-shaped mud-walled hut with thatched roof also known as a *tukul*

Shamma – loosely woven cotton shawl

Tef – indigenous cereal grain; key ingredient of injera

Tej – wine made from honey

Tibbs – pan-fried lamb

Tigrinya – language of Tigray and Birhan's mother tongue

Tella – home-brewed beer made from millet, barley or maize

TPLF – Tigrayan People's Liberation Front